The Political Economy of Normative Trade Power Europe

Arlo Poletti • Daniela Sicurelli

The Political Economy of Normative Trade Power Europe

palgrave
macmillan

Arlo Poletti
Department of Sociology and Social Research
University of Trento
Trento, Italy

Daniela Sicurelli
Department of Sociology and Social Research
University of Trento
Trento, Italy

ISBN 978-3-030-07667-2 ISBN 978-3-319-78864-7 (eBook)
https://doi.org/10.1007/978-3-319-78864-7

Softcover re-print of the Hardcover 1st edition 2018

Printed on acid-free paper

This Palgrave Macmillan imprint is published by the registered company Springer International Publishing AG part of Springer Nature.
The registered company address is: Gewerbestrasse 11, 6330 Cham, Switzerland

Acknowledgement

The research upon which this work is based was made possible by the European Commission [grant number EACEA, 2014–2404].

Contents

List of Acronyms

ACP	African, Caribbean, and Pacific Countries
ASEAN	Association of South East Asian Nations
CA	Central America
CAFTA-DR	Dominican Republic–Central America Free Trade Agreement
CARICOM	Caribbean Community
CARIFORUM	Caribbean Forum
COPA-COGECA	Committee of Professional Agricultural Organizations—General Committee for Agricultural Cooperation in the European Union
CSOs	Civil Society Organizations
DG	Directorate General
EAC	East African Community
EEC	European Economic Community
EPA	Economic Partnership Agreement
ESF	European Services Forum
ETUC	European Trade Union Confederation
EU	European Union
FDI	Foreign Direct Investment
FIDH	International Federation on Human Rights
FOE	Friends of the Earth
FTA	Free Trade Agreement
GATS	General Agreement on Trade in Services
GATT	General Agreement on Tariffs and Trade
GPA	Government Procurement Agreement

GSP	Generalized System of Preferences
GVCs	Global Value Chains
ILO	International Labour Organization
IPE	International Political Economy
IPR	Intellectual Property Rights
ISDS	Investor-State Dispute Settlement
MERCOSUR	Mercado Común del Sur
MFN	Most Favoured Nation
NGO	Non-governmental Organization
OIDHACO	International Office for Human Rights—Action on Colombia
SADC	South African Development Community
SOEs	State-Owned Enterprises
SPSs	Sanitary and Phytosanitary Standards
TBT	Technical Barriers to Trade
TPP	Trans Pacific Partnership
TRIMs	Trade-Related Investment Measures
TRIPs	Agreement on Trade-Related Aspects of Intellectual Property Rights
US	United States
WTO	World Trade Organization

List of Tables

CHAPTER 1

Introduction

Abstract In the last two decades, the European Union (EU) has consistently advocated the use of trade agreements as a means to promote norms and principles such as economic liberalism, sustainable development, and human rights, both globally and towards developing countries. While this stance is in line with the EU's self-representation as an ethical and normative power, it also raises important questions concerning the origins of EU trade policy preferences. Do normative aspirations truly motivate EU trade policy strategies with developing countries? To what extent do these strategies reflect the interests of key domestic constituencies? This chapter offers an overview of the main official documents laying out the normative aspirations of EU trade policy and then introduces the research questions and methodology that guide the subsequent analyses. More generally, the chapter introduces the reader to the book's content: a comparative analysis of the politics underlying the strategy adopted by the EU in the negotiations of comprehensive trade agreements with developing countries since 2010.

Keywords EU trade strategies • norms • interest groups • NGOs

A. Poletti, D. Sicurelli, *The Political Economy of Normative Trade Power Europe*, https://doi.org/10.1007/978-3-319-78864-7_1

1.1 The Normative Aspirations of EU Trade Policy

The European Union (EU) is a pivotal player in international trade relations, holding formidable power *in* trade but also capable of exercising substantial power *through* trade. Trade policy therefore represents a strategic field for the EU to shape its image as a healthy economy and an ethical trade power. In other words, it is an actor committed to using trade agreements in order to promote norms such as economic liberalism, sustainable development, and human rights on a global level.

A brief excursus on trade relations between the EU and developing countries confirms that the Union has constantly striven to demonstrate its leadership in development cooperation and ability to promote norms internationally. Even though the protectionist implications of the Common Agricultural Policy have been a major challenge to its efforts to play an uncontested leadership role in international development throughout its history, it is fair to say that the EU is one of the major architects of programmes seeking to integrate trade and development goals and that it has consistently promoted trade agreements with developing countries that also include a strong normative component. The European Community was the first member of the General Agreement on Tariffs and Trade (GATT) to establish in 1971 a Generalized System of Preferences (GSP) aimed at supporting the process of integration of developing countries into global markets. From 1975 to the early 2000s, it implemented non-reciprocal preferential schemes based on unilateral tariff removal as a form of development cooperation with the African, Caribbean, and Pacific (ACP) countries. Those preferences had been negotiated and agreed upon jointly with the ACP group in the Lomé Conventions.

Since the end of the 1990s, the EU has further reinforced the normative ambition of its trade policy. By negotiating preferential trade agreements (PTAs) with regional blocs of states in South America, East Asia, and the Southern Mediterranean, it deliberately supported processes of regional integration beyond its borders. In so doing it gained the reputation of 'the patron saint of inter-regionalism in international economic relations' (Aggarwal and Fogarty 2006, p. 327). In 2001, the EU also adopted the Everything but Arms initiative, which was conceived to set opportunities for export-led development and contribute to conflict prevention in developing countries. The initiative provides duty-free and quota-free access to all imports to the EU from the least developed countries, with the exception of armaments. Most notably, in the same year, the EU emerged as the most fervent supporter of the Doha Development Agenda, launched in November 2001. In that context the EU promoted a comprehensive multilateral agreement aiming at regulating global free trade while putting developing countries in a condition to take profit from it. Since then, the ambitious goal of supporting trade governance structures that are instrumental to 'managing globalization', that is, integrating market-creating and market-correcting rules, has been the cornerstone of the EU's trade policy strategies at both multilateral and bilateral/regional levels. While promoting a comprehensive multilateral agreement in the Doha Round, in a revision of the GSP, named GSP-plus (which entered into force in 2006), the EU provided additional market access to eligible developing countries, under the condition that those countries ratify, or show progress in the direction of ratifying and implementing, a list of international conventions on human rights, good governance, and sustainable development. The European Commission considered this programme as a 'structural aid measure' aimed at helping developing countries to 'develop their capacities to be involved in the negotiations' (Scheipers and Sicurelli 2008, p. 616).

Even when the EU decided to abandon its 'multilateralism first' approach to trade policy and decided to move more forcefully towards a strategy of trade liberalization through bilateral/regional agreements in 2006 (European Commission 2006), the Union continued to stress the risks that an excessive marketization of the global economy might have for the increasing marginalization of developing countries in the global economy. This rhetoric has survived even in the face of the challenges brought about by the rise of emerging economies (especially the BRICS, i.e. Brazil, Russia, India, China, and South Africa) and the global economic downturn that started in 2007–2008. For one thing, since 2010 the EU has consistently sought to advance a 'deep trade agenda' aimed at removing behind-the-border barriers to trade such as competition policy, public procurement, investments, intellectual property rights (IPR), and technical and sanitary standards in the context of so-called new-generation trade deals with its trading partners (Araujo 2016). However, and in contrast to the PTAs concluded by the US, the Commission's mandates for these negotiations have also consistently included provisions for broad normative and developmental objectives such as the promotion of international law in the fields of labour rights, environmental protection, and human rights.

Recent communications of the European Commission have further elaborated on the image of the EU as an actor committed and able to contribute to development cooperation through trade. The communication of the European Commission (2012) on Trade, Growth, and Development specifies that, while the EU should promote deep trade liberalization through PTAs, it must do so by taking into account the level of development and specific development needs of its negotiating partners. More recently, in a communication ambitiously titled 'Trade for All: Towards a More Responsible Trade and Investment Policy', the European Commission (2015) synthesized the representation of the EU as an ethical trade power, defining its views of the trade–development nexus as one that 'involves using trade agreements and trade preference as levers to promote, around the world, values like sustainable development, human rights, fair and ethical trade and the fight against corruption'. According to the European Commission, this view requires 'a flexible approach' to Free Trade Agreements (FTAs) and 'negotiations to take account of the economic realities of its partners'. In 2016 the Commission (2016) declared a twofold overarching goal, namely, that of fostering economic growth in Europe while, at the same time, promoting development and growth abroad, both in developed and in developing countries.[1] In other words, the EU aims to increase its competitiveness in world trade while acting as a liberal and responsible power. Quoting the rhetoric of the European Commission, 'The EU's success is inextricably bound up with the success of our trading partners, both in the developed and developing world' (*ibidem*).

This solidarity-based and normative discourse used by the EU is consistent with Manners' (2002) representation of the EU as a normative power, namely, as an actor that is structurally bound to promote norms and values beyond its borders. This definition has been widely applied to the analysis of European trade policy (Van den Hoven 2006; Khorana and Garcia 2013; Hirsch 2017). Scholars adopting an approach that focuses on the material interests that underpin the making of EU trade policy, however, criticize this research agenda, claiming that the image of a coherent and effective civilian force for good that pursues a mostly normative foreign policy agenda has no empirical foundations (Young and Peterson 2014). The financial crisis and the growing Euroscepticism have contributed to weakening the heuristic potential of the conceptualization of the EU as a normative power. Yet, the definition of the EU as a normative power still features among the 'key controversies in European integration' in the academic debate (Zimmermann and Dür 2016). As Pollack (2016) observes, recent studies take distance from an uncritical celebration of the normative difference of the EU and investigate, instead, the conditions under which the EU successfully asserts normative leadership. From this perspective, here is still a need for systematic assessments of the EU's normative power aspirations through trade (Carbone and Orbie 2014).

1.2 Research Questions and Methodology

This volume investigates the domestic conditions for the emergence of the EU as a normative power through trade. In doing so, it largely borrows from traditional international political-economy (IPE) approaches, which tend to assume that patterns of political mobilization of organized societal actors largely contribute to shape governments' preferences over trade policy (Hiscox 2001). This approach has been used extensively to analyse US trade policymaking (see Feinberg 2003) and has increasingly gained ground in scholarly investigations of EU trade policy as well (for a review of these approaches, see Poletti and De Bièvre 2014). From this perspective, the European Commission appears largely exposed to industry and civil society pressures in the shaping of its negotiating positions. These analyses have investigated different aspects of EU trade policy, including its role in multilateral trade negotiations (Conceição-Heldt 2011; Poletti 2012; Poletti and De Bièvre 2016), the politics of anti-dumping (Eckhardt 2011), and the politics of PTAs (Dür 2007; Eckhardt and Poletti 2016). These studies, either implicitly or explicitly, all question the validity of approaches that identify in the normative aspirations of the EU the sources of its trade policy strategies.

Despite the relevance of the potential conflict between the self-representation of the EU as a normative trade power and the logic of interest-based political mobilization by key economic constituencies that many studies have considered crucial in defining EU trade policy, surprisingly few studies have systematically subjected to empirical scrutiny whether, and under what conditions, the EU can live up to its normative ambition to use trade policy as a means to support sustainable growth, environmental protection, and human rights in developing countries. There is a lack of explicit treatment in the literature on EU trade policy of theoretical alternatives that might plausibly account for the trade policy outcomes usually explained by referring to the 'normative' character of the EU's role as a global actor. While it is not particularly surprising that traditional political-economy approaches to trade policy tend to do a good job in explaining EU trade relations with trading partners with similar levels of economic, political, and social development, the case of EU trade relations with developing countries deserves special attention. It is precisely in the case of trade relations with developing countries that the potential conflict between the twofold objective of defending the EU's commercial interests and supporting the development needs of trade partners is more likely to emerge. Some studies have tackled this question by focusing on specific instances of EU trade relations with particular sets of developing countries (Heron and Siles-Brügge 2012; Garcia 2015; Siles-Brügge 2014; Eckhardt and Poletti 2016; Hoang and Sicurelli 2017).

Despite the quality of these contributions, only a systematic analysis that compares EU trade policy strategies towards developing countries across different regions and continents will allow for developing propositions that have at least some degree of generalizability on whether, and the conditions under which, the EU deals with the potential conflict between commercial and normative imperatives in its trade policy. This book addresses this challenge, tackling the following questions: What are the objectives that inform the negotiating positions of the EU in PTAs with developing countries? Under what conditions can we expect the EU to adopt an assertive leadership in the promotion of norms through trade? Are EU trade policy strategies with these countries motivated by normative aspirations or are they simply dictated by the preferences and patterns of political mobilization of key domestic constituencies? We aim at addressing these questions by focusing on the positions adopted by the EU in the negotiation of comprehensive trade agreements with developing countries since 2010. To conduct our analysis, we draw inspiration from the excellent contribution by Aggarwal and Fogarty (2004), a study that aims to test the explanatory potential of four competing broad theoretical perspectives—interest group pressures, bureaucratic interests, systemic pressures, and identity politics—for the analysis of EU trade strategies. While broadly following a similar logic, we adapt it to our overarching objective of assessing the relative importance of normative and market imperatives in the shaping of EU trade policy towards developing countries in a period in which, following the deadlock of multilateral trade negotiations under the auspices of the World Trade Organization (WTO), the EU has joined other major trading powers in forcefully seeking to liberalize international trade via bilateral or regional trade agreements.

We use the concept of normative power as a yardstick against which EU trade policymaking can be assessed to critically investigate the relationship between normative and traditional market access concerns in the shaping of policy preferences and negotiation positions of the EU in its trade relations with different sets of developing countries. More precisely, we investigate to what extent the EU fulfils the self-proclaimed goal of integrating market and normative power in the trade negotiations with South American, Sub-Saharan African, and South East Asian countries. We focus on the comprehensive PTAs concluded by the EU since 2009, since they are included in the so-called new-generation trade agreements, namely, those negotiated and initialled after the European Commission's 'Global Europe: Competing in the World' communication (2006). These agreements include those with Peru and Colombia (2011); Central America, CA (2012); the South African Development Community, SADC (2014); West Africa (2014); the East African Community, EAC (2015); and Vietnam (2015). We also include the Economic Partnership Agreement (EPA) with the Caribbean Forum, CARIFORUM (2008), and the FTA with Singapore (2014) in the comparison since they are relevant as precedents to the trade agreements with the ACP and the Association of South East Nations (ASEAN) countries.

For each of those agreements, we test for coherence in the way the Commission has applied the differentiation approach to trade and development. We then trace the politics underlying the EU negotiating position, uncovering the role played by the preferences and patterns of political mobilizations of organized societal interests. In doing so, we aim to develop generalizations on the conditions that push the EU to prioritize normative versus traditional market access considerations in the trade negotiations.

Ultimately, this volume aims at providing both an *evaluation* of the positions taken by the EU in the bilateral trade negotiations and an *explanation* of those positions. On the one hand, we seek to subject to empirical scrutiny whether, and how coherently, EU trade policy strategies live up to the criteria of a normative trade power. In line with the existing literature, we take a pragmatic stance on this issue, and define this benchmark in terms of how much, and how consistently, the EU upholds universal norms and principles in trade agreements. We focus on different sets of such norms, including human rights, sustainable development, but also consider whether the EU grants specific treatment to low- and lower-middle-income countries with respect to traditional tariff concessions. On the other hand, we test competing theoretical explanations to assess whether the negotiating positions of the EU can, or cannot, be plausibly attributed to normative influences. After having mapped EU trade policy strategies, we therefore seek to explain different trade policy strategies and outcomes. A major contribution of our work thus lies in the identification of a number of potential theoretical explanations for observed trade policy strategies. In particular, we explicitly contrast 'normative' arguments about the determinants of EU trade policy preferences with mainstream political-economy approaches to the study of EU trade policy that focus on the material interests and patterns of political mobilization and influence of relevant domestic trade-related constituencies. This contrast between two different sets of potential explanations is meant to clarify what the theoretical boundaries of alternative explanations are, and to provide readers with a systematic view of the theoretical backbone that informs the empirical analyses.

In short, our ambition is both to assess empirically whether broad criteria or 'normative' trade policy towards developing countries are met by the EU and to discriminate between 'normative' and 'interest-based' explanations for observed patterns of trade policymaking. The two aims of the book are closely interlinked. For one, discriminating between theoretical alternatives is important when the position adopted by the EU in each negotiation appears to lack consistency with the declared normative goals of European trade policy. However, even when EU trade strategies happen to be consistent with its self-proclaimed 'normative' character, considering competing explanations can help in overcoming the potential problems of observational equivalence that rise when the same empirical evidence can be used in support of different theoretical perspectives.

The observation that a particular trade policy strategy meets predetermined criteria of a 'normative' trade policy does not suffice to claim that 'normative' concerns of relevant trade-related interests in the EU actually shaped that strategy. Such a trade policy strategy could have been shaped as a result of different causal mechanisms, that is, interest-based preferences of relevant constituencies. Discriminating between alternative explanations of the drivers of EU trade policy preferences is thus crucial both in cases when EU trade policy strategies are not consistent with its self-proclaimed normative ambitions and to empirically isolate interest-based and normative motivations of EU negotiating positions when the two appear to be consistent.

A caveat in our analysis is that we mostly focus on the politics of domestic preferences formation in the EU with respect to the considered international trade negotiations and therefore we do not incorporate an explicit treatment of the bargaining dynamics between the EU and its trading partners. However, a number of important factors contribute to mitigate problems that might arise as a result of our choice. First, our case selection strategy allows us to control for a number of potentially important factors influencing bargaining dynamics. For one, by considering trade agreements between the EU and developing countries we control for the possibility that differences in levels of socio-economic development between the EU and its trading partners might affect bargaining outcomes. In addition, while the countries we consider vary significantly in terms of market size, differentials between them and the EU in terms of market size remain limited, suggesting that the EU's bargaining power should not vary significantly across our cases. Second, the volume considers partner countries' preferences, as well as other relevant trading players' preferences and strategies, as crucial determinants of how EU trade-related interests define their own preferences. For instance, we consider how EU trade strategies with these developing countries are affected by their demands and how they are influenced by the trade strategies of other major trading players such as the US or China.

In order to carry out our analysis, we rely on original empirical data from both primary and secondary sources. We draw empirical evidence on the societal mobilization of interest groups and non-governmental organizations (NGOs) from analyses of policy reports responding to the European Commission consultation exercises. Since informal lobbying often matters more than formal participation of lobbyists in official consultations, we integrate analysis of semi-structured interviews with members of the Commission and relevant stakeholders. We then rely on the method of process tracing to tease out the causal mechanisms that drive the EU's negotiation strategies in the three major sets of case studies analysed. This allows us to weigh the relative explanatory power of different theoretical perspectives on the determinants of EU trade policy strategies, and hence to ascertain under which conditions EU trade policy can indeed be characterized as a 'normative trade policy'.

Our analysis shows that EU trade policy only marginally fulfils the goal of emerging as a norm promoter through trade. More specifically, we show that the relative weight of traditional market access and normative goals in the deals negotiated by the EU varies according to trade relations with the negotiating partners, the participation of those partners in other PTAs, and their integration in the global value chains (GVCs). Thus, the ways in which the EU manages the potential trade-off between normative and traditional market access concerns is by no means exclusively associated with the level of development and specific development needs of its trading partners, as the rhetoric of the European Commission suggests. Shedding light on the impact of preferences and patterns of political mobilization of affected constituencies—both economic interest groups and NGOs—on European trade policy, this analysis stresses the importance of systematically grounding the analysis of 'normative trade power Europe' into broader theories on the political economy of trade policymaking.

1.3 The Structure of the Following Chapters

Chapter 2 aims both to provide a brief description of the institutional and historical contexts within which EU trade policy has developed and to define the broad theoretical context that informs our empirical analyses. First, the chapter offers a brief overview of the formal decision-making procedures through which EU trade policy is made, the role and power of different institutional actors, and how organized societal actors contribute to the shaping of EU positions in trade negotiations. Second, the chapter develops a brief historical overview of the main developments of EU trade policy in the period that precedes our empirical analyses, focusing in particular on the role played in the Doha Round of multilateral negotiations. Finally, and most importantly, the chapter sets out to define the two competing theoretical readings of EU trade policymaking: the first seeing EU trade policy as motivated by normative goals and the second conceiving of it as driven by market access concerns. The chapter explicitly contrasts normative arguments about the determinants of EU trade policy preferences, suggested by constructivist and institutionalist literature, with hypotheses provided by mainstream political-economy approaches to the study of EU trade policy. In this respect, it considers three possible political-economy explanations: traditional market access, domino theory, and GVCs.

Chapters 3, 4, and 5 are devoted to investigating the political-economy dynamics behind the EU positions in the negotiations with Latin American, ACP, and ASEAN countries, respectively. Each chapter first assesses whether trade agreements include provisions that are telling, or not, of a normative trade policy stance, and then traces preferences of relevant trade-related interests (policymakers, business interest groups, and NGOs) to discriminate between alternative explanations. More precisely, Chap. 3 compares the PTAs concluded by the EU and Latin American countries and analyses the role played by European organized societal groups in shaping the EU negotiating position. Chapter 4 focuses on the EPAs concluded with ACP countries. It compares the EPA signed with the CARIFORUM in 2009 with the more recent deals signed with Sub-Saharan African regions. It mainly traces the impact of pressures of development NGOs and of a limited but powerful number of European industries that also mobilized in order to shape the negotiating position of the EU. Chapter 5 compares the only trade agreement concluded so far with an ASEAN developing country, namely, Vietnam (2015), with another trade deal concluded in 2014 with a high-income South East Asian country, namely, Singapore, in order to assess the differential approach of the EU to trade and development cooperation. It investigates the impact of domestic constituencies on the Commission's negotiating position in the negotiations with Vietnam. In order to allow for generalizations, the chapter also reviews the political-economy dynamics behind the ongoing trade negotiations with Malaysia, Indonesia, Thailand, the Philippines, and Myanmar.

The concluding chapter (Chap. 6) takes stock of the findings of each empirical chapter and discusses them in a comparative perspective. It provides an evaluation of the coherence of EU trade and development policies in relations with all developing countries and develops a general discussion of the ways in which the EU prioritizes normative and traditional market access concerns with different sets of developing countries.

Notes

1. The distinction between 'developed' and 'developing' countries is controversial both in the academic context and among actors involved in development cooperation. According to critics, these concepts are the product of wealthy nations' self-centred categorization of states and international relations. In this volume, we acknowledge the limits of these terms, but use them because this classification informs EU trade and development policy. More specifically, we include both low-income countries and middle-lower-income countries in the category of developing countries.

References

Aggarwal, V., and E. Fogarty. 2004. *EU Trade Strategies: Between Regionalism and Globalism*. Basingstoke: Palgrave Macmillan.

———. 2006. The Limits of Interregionalism: The EU and North America. *Journal of European Integration* 27 (3): 327–346.

Araujo, M.B.A. 2016. *The EU Deep Trade Agenda. Law and Policy*. Oxford: Oxford University Press.

Carbone, M., and J. Orbie. 2014. Beyond Economic Partnership Agreements: The European Union and the Trade–Development Nexus. *Contemporary Politics* 20 (1): 1–9.

Conceição-Heldt, E. 2011. *Negotiating Trade Liberalization at the WTO: Domestic Politics and Bargaining Dynamics.* Basingstoke: Palgrave Macmillan.

Dür, A. 2007. EU Trade Policy as Protection for Exporters: The Agreements with Mexico and Chile. *Journal of Common Market Studies* 45 (4): 833–855.

Eckhardt, J. 2011. Firm Lobbying and EU Trade Policy Making: Reflections on the Anti-Dumping Case Against Chinese and Vietnamese Shoes (2005–2011). *Journal of World Trade* 45 (5): 965–991.

Eckhardt, J., and A. Poletti. 2016. Trading with Asia: Import-Dependent Firms and EU-Asia Trade Agreements. *Journal of European Public Policy* 3 (10): 1543–1562.

European Commission. 2006. *Global Europe: Competing in the World.* COM (2006) 567 final, 4 October.

———. 2012. *Trade, Growth and Development Tailoring Trade and Investment Policy for Those Countries Most in Need*, Final Communication to the Parliament, the Council and the European Economic and Social Committee, SEC(2012) 87 Final.

———. 2015. *Trade for All. Towards a More Responsible Trade and Investment Policy.* Communication from the Commission to the European Parliament, the Council, the European Economic and Social Committee and the Committee of the Regions, COM(2015)497/4, 14 October.

———. 2016. *European Position in World Trade.* http://ec.europa.eu/trade/policy/eu-position-in-world-trade/.

Feinberg, R.E. 2003. The Political Economy of United States' Free Trade Arrangements. *The World Economy* 27 (6): 1019–1040.

Garcìa, M. 2013. From Idealism to Realism? EU Preferential Trade Agreement Policy. *Journal of Contemporary European Research* 9 (4): 521–541.

———. 2015. The European Union and Latin America: 'Transformative Power Europe' Versus the Realities of Economic Interests. *Cambridge Review of International Affairs* 28 (4): 621–640.

Heron, T., and G. Siles Brügge. 2012. Competitive Liberalization and the 'Global Europe' Services and Investment Agenda: Locating the Commercial Drivers of the EU–ACP Economic Partnership Agreements. *Journal of Common Market Studies* 50 (2): 250–266.

Hirsch, M. 2017. Identity Matters: The Enforcement of Global Human Rights Treaties by European Union's Trade Instruments. In *International Economic Law and Human Rights*, ed. L. Biukovic and P. Edward Potter. Cheltenham: Edward Publishing.

Hiscox, M.J. 2001. Class Versus Industry Cleavages: Inter-Industry Factor Mobility and the Politics of Trade. *International Organization* 55 (1): 1–46.

Hoang, H.H., and D. Sicurelli. 2017. The EU's Preferential Trade Agreements with Singapore and Vietnam. Market vs. Normative imperatives. *Contemporary Politics* 23 (4): 369–387. https://doi.org/10.1080/13569775.2017.1289303.

Khorana, S., and M. Garcia. 2013. *European Union–India Trade Negotiations: One Step Forward, One Back. Journal of Common Market Studies* 51 (4): 684–700.

Manners, I. 2002. Normative Power Europe: A Contradiction in Terms? *Journal of Common Market Studies* 40 (2): 235–258.

Poletti, A. 2012. *The European Union and Multilateral Trade Governance: The Politics of the Doha Round*. London: Routledge.

Poletti, A., and D. De Bièvre. 2014. The Political Science of European Union Trade Policy: A Literature Review with a Research Outlook. *Comparative European Politics* 12 (1): 101–119.

———. 2016. *Judicial Politics and International Cooperation: From Disputes to Deal-Making at the World Trade Organization*. Colchester: European Consortium for Political Research Press.

Pollack, M. 2016. Living in a Material World: A Critique of Normative Power Europe. In *Key Controversies in European Integration*, ed. H. Zimmermann and A. Dür, 198–204. London and New York: Palgrave.

Scheipers, S., and D. Sicurelli. 2008. Empowering Africa: Normative Power in EU-Africa Relations. *Journal of European Public Policy* 15 (4): 607–623.

Siles-Brügge, G. 2014. *Constructing European Union Trade Policy: A Global Idea of Europe*. London: Palgrave Macmillan.

Van den Hoven, A. 2006. European Union Regulatory Capitalism and Multilateral Trade Negotiations. In *Values and Principles in European Foreign Policy*, ed. S. Lucarelli and I. Manners. London and New York: Routledge.

Young, A., and J. Peterson. 2014. *Parochial Global Europe: 21st Century Trade Politics*. Oxford: Oxford University Press.

Zimmermann, H., and A. Dür, eds. 2016. *Key Controversies in European Integration*. 2nd ed. London and New York: Palgrave.

CHAPTER 2

The EU as a 'Normative' or Traditional 'Market' Trade Power

Abstract Trade policy is among the most prominent policies to be placed under supranational competence of the EU. For this reason, trade negotiations represent a preferential arena for the EU to emerge as a normative leader internationally. This aspiration has affected the positions of the EU both in the Doha Development Round, since 2001, and in the negotiation of PTAs, since 2006. Due to this commitment to norm promotion, constructivist and institutionalist scholars have represented the EU as a distinct player in international relations. From these perspectives, identity and institutional pressures that shape its negotiating positions make it a different actor in the international trade arena, namely, a normative power. On the contrary, mainstream political-economy scholars challenge the representation of the EU as an exceptional actor and tend to conceive of European trade policy as the result of the preferences, patterns of political mobilization, and influence of organized societal groups. These arguments point to the importance of different factors in determining these domestic political processes, including traditional market access concerns, domino effects triggered by the trade policy initiative of the EU's major trade competitors, and different levels of integration in the GVCs with partner countries.

Keywords Trade policy • Normative Power Europe • identity • institutions • political economy

A. Poletti, D. Sicurelli, *The Political Economy of Normative Trade Power Europe*, https://doi.org/10.1007/978-3-319-78864-7_2

2.1 Introduction

Since the origins of the European Community, trade policy has been a supranational competence and the Community has been a full member of the GATT and, since its creation in 1995, of the WTO. Even though the increasing complexity of the issues under negotiation in the WTO have created a conflict of competences within the Union, the EU emerged as a leader of multilateral trade negotiations during the launch of the so-called Doha Development Round in 2001. Since 2006 the EU has also engaged in inter-regional and bilateral trade negotiations, promoting comprehensive agreements aimed at increasing the market potential of the EU and, at the same time, exporting regulatory standards and promoting a model of development based on sustainability standards and human rights.

This normative approach to international trade has raised a number of questions among scholars of international relations. Is the EU emerging as a distinct player in global trade which is institutionally and normatively bound to act as an ethical and ideational power? Is the EU, instead, nothing more than a conventional market power, which ultimately acts in the defence and promotion of its economic interests? How do the normative and strategic dimensions of the EU trade policy coexist and affect its negotiating positions?

In Sect. 2.2 of this chapter, we introduce the decision-making procedures of the EU trade policy and identify the major actors that have a formal role in the definition of the European negotiating positions. Section 2.3 traces the role played by the EU in the Doha negotiations and its main proposals for a multilateral deal. Section 2.4 reviews and discusses the complementary and alternative theoretical approaches emerging in the literature that try to interpret the global role played by the EU throughout the multilateral and bilateral trade negotiations. It discusses institutional and constructivist representations of the EU as a normative power and the perspective of scholars who view EU trade policy as the result of standard political-economy dynamics.

2.2 EU Trade Policy: Actors and Decision-Making Rules

Trade policy is among the most prominent policies to be placed under supranational competence from the very beginning of the European integration process. Following the adoption of the Treaty of Rome in 1957, the European Economic Community (EEC) was granted exclusive competence for the common commercial policy and thus possessed an external personality and held the authority to elaborate, negotiate, and enforce trade relations with the rest of the world (Woolcock 2010a). Over the years the legal competences and the applicable decision-making procedures in the EU trade policy have been the subject of heated political struggles. While, until the adoption of the 1997 Amsterdam Treaty, the original wording of Article 133 (ex-Art. 113 EEC) granting the Community exclusive competences for the EU's common commercial policy remained substantially unchanged, the expansion of the international trade agenda to the so-called new trade issues (concerning services, IPR, technical barriers to trade [TBTs], sanitary and phytosanitary standards [SPSs], and investments), formalized with the creation of the WTO in 1995, put political–administrative strain on the Community's legal trade competences. The ensuing political struggle between the Commission and the member states concerning who should have the ultimate competence in these 'new trade issues' led to the redefinition of the EU trade policymaking rules in subsequent treaty revisions (Poletti and De Bièvre 2014b), which is widely documented by scholarly research (Meunier 2003; Meunier and Nicolaïdis 1999; Nicolaïdis and Meunier 2002; Woolcock 2000; Young 2000).

The adoption of the Treaty of Lisbon in 2009 sought to clarify many important aspects of the legal and procedural aspects of EU trade that previous rounds of treaty revisions had failed to streamline effectively. A brief description of the Treaty's relevant provisions and of the political dynamics that they have engendered can therefore help in understanding how the trade policy in the EU is made, who the relevant actors are, and how they interact in the context of international trade negotiations.

The Lisbon Treaty is important because it concludes the long-standing debate by confirming that all the key aspects of external trade, including all services, trade-related IPR, and, most importantly, foreign direct investment (FDI), will henceforth come under exclusive EU competence (Woolcock 2010b). Exclusive competence means that the formal basis for decision-making is qualified majority voting. Although all services fall under EU competence, the Lisbon Treaty includes provision for the use of unanimity in some politically sensitive sectors. Pressure from a number of member states, backed by public service unions in the health, education, and social services sectors, led to special provisions in Article 207 (4) requiring unanimity when the agreements being negotiated risk prejudicing linguistic and cultural diversity or when they risk disturbing the national organization of the health, education, and social services (Woolcock 2010a).

This discussion introduces the important distinction between the so-called regular trade agreements and so-called mixed trade agreements. The former include issues that fall squarely under EU exclusive competences, while the latter include issues either requiring unanimity or falling into member states' competences. As we explain in detail below, this distinction has important consequences for decision-making, yet it should be noted that in recent years the trade agreements negotiated and adopted by the EU have been so broad in scope that member states have often been inclined to consider them as mixed agreements.

On the basis of the Lisbon Treaty, the decision-making process for the negotiation and conclusion of bilateral, regional, and multilateral trade agreements is as follows. First, the Commission drafts a mandate for new negotiations, which is then presented to the Council and the European Parliament. The mandate is adopted by a Council decision, formally by qualified majority voting but usually by consensus, which authorizes the opening of negotiations and sets the negotiating directives for the Commission. For 'mixed agreements' further approval by the representatives of member states' governments in a meeting with the council is necessary. The European Parliament is informed about the mandate and can comment on it, but formally its approval is not required. Then Commission negotiates on behalf of the EU, and throughout the negotiations it reports regularly to both the Council and the European Parliament's Committee on International Trade.

The rules for approval of the agreement change, again, depending on the type of agreement. In the case of 'regular agreements', approval comes in the form of a Council decision by qualified majority and by the European Parliament by simple majority. As stated before, however, the tendency has been for 'mixed' agreements, which implies that they must be signed and ratified by the EU and all 28 member states according to their own constitutional requirements, a tendency based on the legal argument that those trade agreements include provisions that still fall under the competences of the member states and not of the Union. The political reason is that the mixed nature of these agreements leads to a de facto veto right for member states, since they can refuse to sign or ratify the agreement (Van der Loo and Pelkmans 2016).

Finally, it should be noted that, apart from the decision-making authorities with the formal legal authority to decide, private interests and civil society organizations (CSOs) also crucially affect the making of EU trade policy. These associations have both formal and informal channels of influence in the policy process. Domestic interest groups lobby their national ministers to shape the Council's position. The European Commission has the discretion to open online consultations and organize round tables with stakeholders in which these groups can express their positions on the issues under negotiation. These associations can also push forward their demands through informal contact with the staff of the Commission and members of the European Parliament. Indeed, these organized societal groups of different kinds provide critical resources that EU policymakers need in the framing of this important policy, such as information, expertise, and political support.

2.3 The EU and the Doha Round

Given the highly supranational character of the European trade policy, the EU has been able to act as a unitary player in the GATT–WTO rounds. While it followed the US leadership in the GATT rounds, in 2001 it emerged as the main promoter of the Doha Development Round.

Since the inception of the GATT in 1947, the structure of reciprocal concessions in multilateral trade rounds has been the cornerstone of the multilateral trade regime. Trade rounds for a long time have consisted essentially of a series of deals aimed at lowering and eliminating the tariffs to trade in industrial goods through reciprocal concessions. In the early phase of the GATT system, reciprocal tariff reduction agreements consisted of deals struck bilaterally on a product-by-product basis (Gowa and Kim 2005; Jupille et al. 2013). Bilateral agreements on market access were then extended to all the members of the trade regime by virtue of the most favoured nation (MFN) clause. In the early phase of the GATT, the decision-making logic was therefore bilateral, whereas the policy outcomes were multilateral (Martin 1992).

One of the most important features of the evolution of the multilateral trading system concerns the expansion of its scope to include regulatory issues. As the multilateral trading system proved to be incredibly successful in reducing the average tariff barriers to trade in manufactured goods, the members of the trade regime started to realize that significant barriers to trade persisted in the form of distinct domestic regulatory practices. As a result, the international trade agenda gradually started to expand to the realm of regulatory issues that traditionally had been within the boundaries of domestic governance to ensure that domestic rules could not become substitutes for tariffs and quotas (Holmes 2006). While the issue of non-tariff barriers first appeared on the international trade agenda during the Tokyo Round (1973–1979), it was the Uruguay Round (1986–1994) that marked a real qualitative leap in the nature of cooperation in the trade regime (Woolcock 2000). With such negotiations the WTO member states expanded the scope of the WTO rules to include commitment to the liberalization of trade in services (General Agreement on Trade in Services—GATS), the protection of trade-related aspects of intellectual property rights (TRIPS), the discriminatory trade effects of domestic standards (TBTs), the application of SPSs, and investments (trade-related investment measures—TRIMs).

In addition to broadening the scope of the multilateral trade regime's action, the Uruguay Round also marked a change in the ways in which multilateral trade rules would be agreed. Until the launch of the Uruguay Round in 1986, the GATT rounds were characterized by the separation of issues into discrete negotiations, ranging from negotiations on a product-by-product basis to negotiations on linear tariff cuts for all products within broad sectors and negotiations on the adoption of regulatory standards. In 1986, with the launch of the Uruguay Round, the members of the trade regime decided that the launching, implementation, and outcome of negotiations would be treated as a 'single undertaking' in which negotiations on the different issues would be bound into a single package via the 'nothing is agreed until everything is agreed' rule (Croome 1999).

With the successful conclusion of the Uruguay Round, however, the capacity of the multilateral trade regime to perform its legislative function seems to have ground to a halt. The Uruguay Round planted the seed for further liberalization commitments to take place within a short time span. To mitigate the concerns of those WTO members who were aware of the limited potential for agricultural trade liberalization of the Uruguay Round Agreement on Agriculture, the text included a so-called built-in agenda (Article 20) mandating WTO members to start a new round of negotiations on agriculture by the end of 1999. Similarly, it was clear to negotiators that the GATS architecture and commitments were only the first step towards meaningful liberalization of trade in services, and, as a result, further negotiations on services were provided for by a clearly defined time schedule (Bohmer and Glania 2003). In 1999 the members of the WTO gathered in Seattle to launch a new round of multilateral trade negotiations. Besides the so-called built-in agenda for further liberalization of agricultural and services trade, it was clear that these negotiations were to include a set of new commitments in a wide range of regulatory areas. The EU was particularly adamant in its intention to broaden the agenda of the new Millennium Round to a wide array of regulatory issues (Baldwin 2006; Falke 2005; Van den Hoven 2002; Young and Peterson 2006). Afterwards, the Uruguay Round Commissioner Lamy gave shape to the so-called multilateralism first approach to EU trade policy, putting in place a moratorium on bilateral trade agreements (Elsig 2007), while sponsoring broad-based negotiations embodied in the doctrine of managed globalization (Meunier 2007).

In the preparatory document for the Seattle WTO Ministerial Conference, the European Commission (1999) argued that the new round should aim not only to open markets in agriculture, manufacturing, services, and free electronic commerce but also to regulate a new host of domestic regulatory policies (Deutsch 2001; Young et al. 2000). For instance, the EU proposed negotiations on intellectual property (especially on indications of the geographical origin of agricultural products), TBTs, and trade defence measures' reform (Deutsch 2001). Furthermore, the EU strongly advocated the inclusion of the so-called Singapore issues on the negotiation agenda: competition, trade facilitation, public procurement, and investments. According to the EU, new rules on FDI would provide more unequivocal protection for investors and avoid bidding wars between governments aiming to attract FDIs as well as simplifying and complementing the existing panoply of bilateral investment agreements while not putting developing countries at a structural disadvantage in relation to large, advanced, industrialized countries (De Bièvre 2006). The EU also argued that greater transparency in public procurement and the simplification of customs valuation procedures would enhance efficiency, facilitate trade, increase foreign market access, reduce corruption, and contribute to the economic development of developing countries (Woolcock 2005). An agreement on trade facilitation was deemed necessary to facilitate trade through the reduction of the administrative burden (Woolcock 2000). In competition policy the EU asked WTO member states to negotiate rules against private cartel practices and rules on how the activities of competition authorities could be coordinated. Finally, the EU also advocated that the liberalization agreements concluded under the WTO should be linked to commitments to minimum environmental and labour standards (Deutsch 2001).

The Seattle Ministerial Conference ended up as a failure, witnessing the vociferous street protests of anti-globalist movements and exposing significant differences among member countries concerning what should be on the WTO agenda as well as shortcomings in the manner in which the WTO conducts its business and interacts with other international organizations and NGOs (Schott 2000). Among the many reasons for the Seattle failure, developing countries' newly found assertiveness and their opposition to the inclusion of the Singapore issues and scepticism towards making commitments in the areas of environmental and labour standards were certainly prominent. In addition, with the election of the Bush administration, the politics of trade changed. As the Bush administration was less beholden to those domestic interest groups that were critical of trade liberalization and the globalization of American business, such as unions and environmental groups, the US returned to a purely market-access-based agenda that would eschew the new issues, such as trade and labour and trade and the environment (Falke 2005, p. 12).

Against this background an agreement for the launch of a new round of multilateral trade negotiations was finally reached in the Doha WTO ministerial meeting in November 2001. The agreement was undoubtedly facilitated by the commonly perceived need to send a signal of unity after the terrorist attacks against the US that had taken place only two months previously (Blustein 2009). The Doha Declaration (WTO 2001) set out an ambitious negotiating agenda. In addition to a commitment to liberalize trade further in agriculture, services, and non-agricultural products, to regulate further the trade-related aspects of IPR, and to clarify the WTO rules on anti-dumping and subsidies as well as on regional trade agreements and special and differential treatment, WTO members states decided to start discussions on the establishment of new rules and commitments in areas such as trade and environment, technical assistance, and capacity building. In addition, all four Singapore issues were included as negotiating topics in the Doha Declaration. In sum, starting in November 2001, WTO member states engaged in a new round of trade negotiations that both set out an ambitious liberalizing agenda for traditional market access issues and further expanded the potential for the WTO to spur positive integration in a wide array of issue areas that traditionally had been regulated at the domestic level.

The EU has been one of the most fervent supporters of this broad-based agenda. Throughout these negotiations the EU consistently and simultaneously pursued different types of trade policies, ranging from traditional market access issues to so-called social trade policies (Meunier and Nicolaïdis 2006; Poletti 2012; Young 2007). This means that the political processes underlying the EU trade negotiating position in the Doha Round varied considerably. In some cases they played out in a fairly narrow policy community including national and EU officials and relatively few economic interests, while in other instances they were characterized by more contested and politicized types of interactions, witnessing the participation of organizations representing diffuse interests. Additionally, the positions taken by the EU in a number of areas can hardly be described as being driven by purely rational and self-interested motivations, since the EU strongly supported the 'development' dimension of the Doha Round, sided with developing countries on key matters, such as access to medicines, and, more generally, showed itself to be quite responsive to the concerns of a wide array of organized societal actors pursuing value-based agendas in certain issue areas (Poletti 2013).

Despite these ambitions, the Doha Round failed to produce a significant move forward in multilateral trade liberalization. Since the very beginning, it became clear that the capacity of global trade powers, such as the EU and the US, no longer sufficed to secure a multilateral trade deal. The negotiation assertiveness of middle-income developing countries, such as Brazil, India, and to a lesser extent China, had reduced the room for these global trade players to export their preferred policies to the WTO framework. Immediately after the launch of the Doha Round in 2001, an aggregation process of previously diverging negotiating approaches of a number of developing countries took place. This process culminated in the failure of the Cancun WTO Ministerial Conference in 2003, when the so-called G20 group of countries opposed a deal on agriculture that was proposed jointly by the EU and the US and forced the EU to drop the Singapore issues from the negotiating agenda. This experience made it clear that middle-income developing countries were ready to exert negotiating power and therefore that their positions were to be considered fully part of the equation for any future deal in the multilateral trade arena. In various subsequent critical moments, it became even clearer that the ambitions of negotiating parties had to be scaled down dramatically if an agreement was to be reached, and in the end WTO members could only find common ground on an important yet minor issue, such as trade facilitation. Thus, the ambitious process that started in Doha in 2001 ultimately boiled down to the 2013 Bali Trade Facilitation Agreement, which entered into force on 22 February 2017 following its ratification by two-thirds of the WTO membership. The Trade Facilitation Agreement has the potential to generate significant benefits for all the WTO members in that it contains provisions for expediting the movement, for the release and clearance of goods, including goods in transit, and for effective cooperation between customs and other appropriate authorities on trade facilitation and customs compliance issues. However, the agreement represents a dramatic scaling down of the initial attempts to push forward an ambitious agenda for the further liberalization of trade in agricultural and manufactured goods and services as well as for further regulatory cooperation in a wide array of issue areas.

The reasons for this crisis of the WTO's legislative function are numerous. In addition to the new assertiveness of the emerging powers, the increased heterogeneity of WTO members' preferences due to the rising number of member states, the politicization of trade policymaking brought about by the inclusion of regulatory issues on the WTO's agenda, and the reluctance to commit to agreements that would have had a highly binding character due to the reform of the Dispute Settlement Mechanism have also all been considered as key factors in explaining the stalemate of multilateral trade deal making (Poletti and De Bièvre 2016).

In this context the EU soon started to come to terms with the possibility that the Doha Round would not produce significant results. This became particularly clear between 2005 and 2006 when the EU realized that an agreement on the liberalization of agricultural trade was not in sight, despite the EU having made considerable efforts to meet the demands of the key developing countries (Poletti et al. 2015). This produced a shift in the EU's broader trade policy orientation. Even though it was confronted with difficulties in the early phase of negotiations, the EU held the official line that it was entirely dedicated to multilateralism and would maintain its moratorium on negotiating PTAs. In the middle of the 2000s, however, the EU finally admitted defeat and radically reversed course. In 2006 the European Commission released its 'Global Europe. Competing in the World' communication, which announced a marked shift in the EU trade strategy from a 'multilateralism first' approach to a more strategic approach based on bilateralism (Elsig 2007). EU policymakers realized that their multilateral bargaining power had waned and that the deadlock of the Doha Round was unlikely to be resolved any time soon, and it embarked on a number of so-called FTA negotiations with a wide array of important partners. Many of the regulatory issues that the EU had sought in vain to include in a Doha package thus became the subject of bilateral or regional agreements.

2.4 The EU as a Normative Power Through Trade

Within the constructivist and institutional literature, a number of scholars interpret the attempt of the EU to emerge as a leader in the Doha Round and to promote regulatory standards and a development-oriented approach to trade since 2006 as a manifestation of its normative power.

Since the end of the Cold War, the EU has represented itself as an ethical power in its international relations, engaged in promoting norms beyond its borders. Its ambition of promoting norms internationally has emerged in the context of the EU trade policy especially since the early 2000s. The EU has tried to lead the Doha Round with the aim of shaping a development-friendly image of the WTO.

After the publication of the 'Global Europe: Competing in the World' communication (European Commission 2006), the EU also promoted inter-regional and bilateral negotiations aimed at concluding comprehensive trade agreements promoting trade and investment liberalization as well as regulatory standards, the rule of law, sustainable development, and human rights. Studies belonging to constructivist and institutionalist research programmes share the representation of the EU as a normative power through trade but provide different explanations for its normative agenda. Constructivists focus on the impact of the ideational structure of the EU on its trade policy and propose an identity politics explanation, which suggests that the constitutive values and principles of the EU shape its conceptions of what is appropriate and legitimate in international relations and contribute to defining its interests in the trade negotiations. Institutionalists, instead, claim that the distribution of power between the European institutions involved in trade policymaking has empowered actors committed to norm promotion and therefore has set the incentives for the emergence of a normative trade policy.

These explanations are complementary, and many analyses of EU trade policy actually integrate the insights of the two approaches. They share a representation of the EU as a unique actor in international trade, which, in contrast to traditional market powers, is structurally bound to act as a normative power (Sicurelli 2016). Arguably, within both the identity politics and the institutionalist school, there is a debate on the extent to which the EU acts as a coherent normative power and an exceptional actor in international relations. In the following sections, we focus on the constructivist and institutionalist literature that tries to explain the normative agenda of the EU trade policy while acknowledging that the debate has recently focused on the conditions that either facilitate or constrain the efforts of the EU to emerge as a normative power.

2.4.1 *Identity Pressures for Norm Promotion*

Manners (2002) first uses the term Normative Power Europe to represent a distinctive feature of the EU as an actor that is committed to shaping what is normal in international relations and is at least relatively able to do so. According to the author, the history of the construction of the EU as a political entity and its own constitutive norms have set the conditions for the emergence of its international identity as a normative power. Due to the distinctive features of European integration as an elite-driven project based on a legal order, the Union has built its own identity primarily on the norms that constitute its treaties, namely, peace, liberty, democracy, rule of law, human rights, social solidarity, anti-discrimination, sustainable development, and good governance. Whitman (2011) synthetizes the identity origins of Normative Power Europe, claiming that the EU *is* a normative actor and *acts* in a normative way in its international relations. Lucarelli (2006) further elaborates on the mutually constitutive relationship between the identity, the discourse, and the foreign policy of the EU. From this perspective the constitutive norms of the EU shape the rhetorical discourse of European leaders. The official discourse of European institutions, in turn, limits the room for *manoeuvre* of EU policymakers, since it affects their self-perception and ultimately their interests.

Building on these contributions, several empirical studies find evidence of the identity of the Union as a normative power through trade. Van den Hoven (2006) suggests that the proactive role played by the EU in the Doha Round can be interpreted as a manifestation of the attempt of the Union to promote its own values and principles beyond its borders. By proposing a comprehensive multilateral agreement, which would tackle a broad agenda of trade, investment, and regulatory issues, including investment, competition, transparency rules, and sustainable development, the EU has tried to promote the regulatory approach to trade that it has adopted internally. Van den Hoven acknowledges that the EU had a commercial interest in promoting a comprehensive round, since that would allow it to negotiate concessions from its negotiating partners as compensation for its removal of barriers to trade in agriculture and textiles. Nevertheless, he stresses that economic interests alone do not explain the commitment of the EU to norm promotion through multilateral negotiations. According to the author, there is a strong identity component behind the negotiating position of the EU, since the EU only defended its interests in the trade negotiations when it believed that there were value- and principle-based arguments in support of those interests. From this perspective even the positions of the EU that raised more critical reactions in the Doha negotiations, namely, those concerning agricultural policy, can be interpreted through ideational lenses. As a matter of fact, the EU has reduced spending on trade-distortive subsidies and only maintained those subsidies that promote ideas and norms concerning environmental protection, sustaining rural economies, and providing farmers with reasonable incomes.

Other authors demonstrate that the normative approach pursued by the EU in its international relations can even undermine its commercial interests. Riddervold (2010) observes that the EU has played a leading role in the making of a Consolidated Maritime Labour Convention in the context of the International Labour Organization (ILO) by promoting high standards of human rights protection and strict control measures, even though those norms will eventually increase the costs for both European ship owners and national administrations. According to the author, this rights-driven approach pursued by the EU in this context is the expression of conceptions of legitimate behaviour that are consolidated among European institutions and member states. Sjursen and Rosén (2017) also emphasize the prevailing of normative considerations over commercial interests in their analysis of the EU sanctions against Russia in response to the Ukrainian crisis in 2015. The authors observe that the EU member states were able to agree on a common reaction to the crisis, even though such a response risked undermining the substantial trade, investment, and financial interests of key member states, including Germany and the UK, which feared Russian retaliation measures.

From this perspective, identity considerations also motivate the positions adopted by the EU in the negotiation of PTAs. Hirsch (In press) interprets the commitment of the EU to human rights promotion in the context of PTAs as being strongly influenced by the collective identity of the EU and of its perceived social role as a norm promoter. His study shows that the conditionality measures included in the EU GSP-plus and the human rights clauses promoted by the EU in the negotiation of PTAs are the expression of a logic of identity and of the aspiration of the EU to build its identity as a human rights promoter worldwide. The identity basis of the EU trade policy, according to the author, indicates that its human rights approach to trade policy is relatively durable over time. Khorana and Garcia (2013) highlight the distinct feature of the EU as a normative power emerging in the ongoing trade negotiations with India, in which the EU's principled stance on human rights promotion clashed with the realist conceptualization of international relations pursued by the Indian Government. In this context the EU insisted on subordinating the conclusion of the trade agreement to furthering the dialogue between the two parties on human rights, with an emphasis on the human rights implications of the Indian-occupied Kashmir. The EU has pursued this rights-based approach to trade negotiations despite the firm opposition of its Indian counterpart, in so doing risking undermining the success of the negotiations.

While sharing with those scholars an ideational approach to the EU trade policy, Orbie (2011), Orbie and Khorana (2015), Rosamond (2014), and Siles-Brügge (2014) adopt more critical perspectives. Siles-Brügge (2014) focuses on the role of neoliberal ideas and discourse in shaping the EU trade policy and notes that, by referring to the globalization of economic constraints, the European Commission has engaged in strategic use of discourse aimed at legitimating controversial neoliberal policies. In the context of the negotiation of the EPAs with the ACP states, this neoliberal argument has motivated EU pressures for WTO-plus liberalization commitments, despite the opposition voiced by its negotiating partners. Rosamond (2014) also observes a potential conflict between the constitutive principles of the EU. The policy prescriptions deriving from the principle of economic liberalism, which is a core constitutive principle of the EU that has largely been overlooked by the literature on Normative Power Europe, are potentially at odds with other principles, inspired by a cosmopolitan view of liberalism, such as human rights, sustainable development, and good governance. This normative conflict may lead to a lack of coherence in the way in which the EU exports its norms internationally. Orbie (2011) and Orbie and Khorana (2015) also observe tension between the EU's promotion of deep liberalization commitments, on the one hand, and its commitment to exporting cosmopolitan liberalism norms, on the other, which implies an interventionist stance in the trade negotiations.

A recent group of works identifies in the political mobilization of CSOs, opposing what they perceive as potentially unacceptably 'disembedding outcomes' of the ongoing EU trade policy negotiations, a key driver of the normative character of the EU trade policy. De Ville (2016), De Ville and Siles-Brügge (2016), and Young (2016), for instance, view the politics of the Transatlantic Trade and Investment Partnership (TTIP) as entirely new, because, due to the regulatory scope of its provisions and thus their potential to intrude into domestic politics and undermine contracting parties' ability to regulate the market to promote fundamental social values in the pursuit of the general interest, CSOs were able to bring to bear their value-based opposition to the prospective agreement. Thus, according to this line of reasoning, the politics of the TTIP presents a challenge for EU trade policy scholars and points to the need to draw attention to the increasing importance of value-based concerns about the legitimacy of the EU trade policy raised by a set of newly mobilized societal actors that thus exceeds an assessment based on criteria of economic efficiency.

2.4.2 *Institutional Incentives for Norm Promotion*

In support of constructivist studies that depict the EU as a normative power, a group of scholars belonging to the institutionalist school claims that the distribution of power within the EU and the procedures that regulate EU policymaking make the Union prone to pursue a normative trade policy.

Manners (2002) elaborates on the link between institutions and identity in the EU and claims that its hybrid structure, consisting of intergovernmental and supranational institutions, makes it prone to act differently from sovereign states and 'pre-disposes it to act in a normative way' (Manners 2002, p. 242). Building on this premise, one can expect that trade policy, which is one of the most supranational policies of the Union, is a preferential venue for norm diffusion. In support of this hypothesis, Meunier (2005) specifies that, since the Rome Treaty, the delegation of policymaking powers from the intergovernmental level (the governments of the member states) to the supranational level (the European Commission) has had the effect of insulating the trade policy from protectionist pressures and, as a result, promoting trade liberalization internationally (Meunier 2005).

Meunier and Nicolaïdis (2006) provide a more conflictual, but, nonetheless, normative, image of the EU trade policy. They argue that such a delegation of powers does not prevent a collision between the Commission and the Council in the shaping of a European negotiating position. Paradoxically, though, according to the authors, this conflict ultimately strengthens the role of the EU as a 'power through trade', namely, a power that is able to use trade as an instrument to promote norms beyond its borders. This argument is based on two assumptions. Firstly, the size of the EU's market represents a formidable resource of power that puts the EU in a position to promote comprehensive trade agreements. Secondly, the need of European institutions and member states to reach a consensus on a negotiating position compels the European Commission to try to accommodate those heterogeneous preferences. As a result, not only free trade proponents and protectionists but also principle-based arguments will be incorporated into the negotiating position of the EU. The EU can use the conflict between European institutions strategically as a bargaining chip for promoting regulatory barriers, including social and environmental clauses, in the trade agreements with countries that are not members of the Union.

A number of empirical studies also confirm the relationship between the institutional system of the EU and its role as a norm promoter through trade. Larsén (2007) remarks on the representation of EU trade policymaking as conflictual and finds that conflict over trade policymaking takes place even between different Directorate Generals (DGs) of the Commission involved in the shaping of the European position. The choice to locate the European Commission negotiating team with DG Development rather than DG Trade in the context of the negotiations between the EU and South Africa (concluded in 1999) was crucial for determining the EU agenda and the outcome of the negotiations and shows that DG Development has played a relevant role in pursuing a developmentally oriented trade agreement. Bossuyt (2009) contends that the ambitious position of the EU in promoting human and labour rights through PTAs with Asia and Latin American countries is motivated by a mix of factors, including the bureaucratic interests of DG Trade in expanding its role in the social sphere, the goal of increasing foreign policy coherence, and a strong concern about the legitimacy of the EU trade policy.

The signing of the Lisbon Treaty in 2009 further raised expectations among scholars of a growing normative role of the Union in the context of trade policy. Firstly, the treaty further strengthened the supranational dimension of the European trade policy by reducing the areas of mixed competences and bringing investment under the exclusive competence of the Union (Woolcock 2010b). Secondly, it increased the powers of the European Parliament over trade policymaking. While, under the Nice

Treaty, the European Commission had the discretion to consult the Parliament during the trade negotiations, under the Lisbon Treaty, formal consultations of the Parliament are required. Most notably, the Parliament has gained assent power over the final trade agreement. Studies of the impact of the European Parliament on the trade policy demonstrate that the institutional incentives for norm promotion have increased under the Lisbon Treaty due to the strengthening of the European Parliament as a veto player. Feliu and Serra (2015) claim that, despite the different sensitivities to human rights held by members of Parliament from different nationalities and political groupings, the European Parliament represents a normative voice within the EU and its strengthened powers have increased the pressure for the EU to act as a normative power. As empirical support for this statement, Ripoll Servent (2014) notes that the Parliament's veto against the Anti-Counterfeiting Trade Agreement in 2012 confirms its ability to reject a trade agreement if it does not prioritize human rights promotion. Furthermore, Larsén's (2017) study of the ongoing negotiations between the EU and India demonstrates that the European Parliament, by promoting cooperation on human rights between the two parties, has influenced the European position and affected the negotiating dynamics.

Like in the constructivist school, a number of institutionalist studies are also cautious about the representation of the EU as a coherent norm promoter. Among these studies, Conceição-Heldt and Meunier (2014) claim that, even in the case of trade policy, which is mostly under EU competence, the Union fails to act as a cohesive actor, which undermines the coherence and effectiveness of its role as a norm promoter. Similarly, Young and Peterson (2014) demonstrate that the multiple veto players involved in the EU trade policymaking and the conflict between the liberal-oriented European Commission and protectionist member states tend to water down the normative provisions in the fields of development and human rights in the trade agreements concluded by the EU.

These contributions show that there is an ongoing lively debate on the relationship between identity, institutions, and the role of the EU as a normative power. These studies raise a fundamental question concerning the conditions under which the institutional and ideational structure of the EU contributes to strengthening its normative ambition. Political-economy accounts of EU policymaking contribute to this debate and try to address this question.

2.5 Mainstream Political-Economy Perspectives on the EU Trade Policy

Recent studies increasingly analyse the EU trade policy through the lenses of standard IPE approaches to trade policy (Poletti and De Bièvre 2014a). In line with these approaches, they tend to use the EU as an empirical case to test and develop theories that conceive of the trade policy orientation of governments as being determined by the anticipated distributional implications of the expected policies and the patterns of political mobilization that these engender among organized societal actors. The assumption underlying most of these works is that political actors act as office seekers and have strong incentives to anticipate the reaction of societal groups—especially producer groups—and to avoid policies that will weaken their chances of re-election or reappointment (De Bièvre and Dür 2005).

While early works focus almost exclusively on the role of organized business groups and overlook the preferences and patterns of the political mobilization of CSOs, assuming these latter actors' inability to overcome collective action problems (De Bièvre 2014; Dür and De Bièvre 2007), more recent literature analyses the conditions under which diffuse interests, such as CSOs can overcome collective action problems and play a key role in the politics of trade. These studies show that businesses and CSOs can indeed act together to defend particular material interests, particularly when regulatory issues are at stake, when the issues are perceived as being publicly salient, or when a few organized groups skilfully manage to raise their public saliency (Dür and Mateo 2014; Poletti and De Bièvre 2014b; Poletti and Sicurelli 2016; Pollack and Shaffer 2009; Young and Peterson 2006). Examples of CSOs and businesses joining forces in the context of the WTO Doha Round and bilateral trade agreements also abound in the EU trade policy literature (De Bièvre et al. 2016; Kelemen 2010; Poletti and Sicurelli 2012, 2016; Young 2004; Young and Peterson 2006). Despite significant differences in the causal mechanisms that they postulate, these works concur in characterizing EU trade policymaking as a policy process 'from below', namely, one that is largely driven by patterns of political mobilization of organized domestic constituencies, which interact with EU institutional opportunity structures to produce particular trade policy outcomes in the EU. These works, which focus on the material interests of organized societal groups in the EU, largely fall into three broad categories. While these three sets of arguments all concur in describing the EU trade policy as the outcome of a political battle between those favouring and those opposing a particular policy initiative, they advance different views on the types of causal mechanisms that drive such political conflicts. In the remainder we provide a brief overview of these broad sets of arguments and review how they have been used to account for particular EU trade policy initiatives.

2.5.1 *Traditional Market Access Concerns*

Standard IPE models of trade policy traditionally assume this policy to engender a political conflict pitting export-oriented against import-competing sectors (Hiscox 2001). The first set of actors stands to gain from the increased market access opportunities that trade liberalization can bring about, while the second stands to lose from them because of the greater exposure to foreign competition in domestic markets that it can generate. Assuming that policymakers have no independent trade policy preferences and have an interest in catering to the demands of these groups to enhance their chances of re-election or reappointment, this view posits that trade policy choices are ultimately the result of the lobbying efforts and competition for influence of these organized groups. Examples of the application of this model of trade policy to the analysis of the EU trade policy abound (Poletti and De Bièvre 2014a). De Bièvre and Dür (2005), for instance, show how the delegation of trade policy authority to agents in the EU serves the purpose of simultaneously defending the interests of export-oriented producers seeking the opening up of foreign markets and the interests of import-competing groups seeking protection from increased foreign import penetration in the EU market. Dür (2008) and Poletti (2011, 2012) similarly find support for the claim that the EU negotiating positions in different rounds of multilateral trade negotiations were largely determined by interest groups' pressure, showing that in these instances there were striking parallels between the positions defended by economic interests and the public actors' choices. Similarly, Dür and De Bièvre (2007) find strong evidence in support of collective action theory in their assessment of the influence of organizations representing diffuse interests within the EU on the occasion of negotiations concerning the EPAs.

These dynamics are by no means confined to the realm of multilateral trade negotiations. Heron and Siles-Brügge (2012) find evidence that the trade preferences of firms seeking to secure 'first-mover' advantages in highly regulated service markets were key drivers of the recent proliferation of bilateral and regional trade agreements signed by the EU. In particular, these domestic-societal preferences were reflected in the EU's bilateral services and investment agenda and, more tangibly, in agreements including the EU–CARIFORUM EPA and the EU–Korea FTA. In a similar vein, Siles-Brügge (2014) makes a convincing case that the EU subordinated the developmental to the commercial imperative in its trade negotiations with ACP countries, refocusing its trade preferences to increase its offensive leverage in the ongoing trade negotiations with these countries. Recent studies on the EU politics of the TTIP also show that EU negotiators have consistently sought to defend the interests of organized domestic business constituencies with respect to the elimination of traditional tariffs to trade. Dür and Lechner (2015) find that requests for tariff cuts appear quite consistently in all the business sectors considered and rank as the third most important issue brought to the attention of public policymakers. Young (2016) finds that substantial concerns about tariff concessions and market access more generally have been raised on both sides of the Atlantic by farm groups, service providers, and steel manufacturers.

These dynamics of political mobilization are not restricted to negotiations concerning traditional barriers to trade, such as tariffs and quotas. The politics of regulatory cooperation, the so-called deep trade agenda (Young and Peterson 2006), has become an increasingly important feature of international trade policymaking at all levels, multilateral, bilateral, and regional. It is widely documented that the politics of international regulatory cooperation can also be expected to be highly politically charged given the potentially severe adjustment costs that regulatory harmonization can bring about for domestic firms (De Bièvre et al. 2014). Just as in the case of negotiations concerning traditional trade liberalization, trade negotiations on regulatory issues also engender a political conflict between domestic organized groups either seeking to accrue the benefits of such an initiative or seeking to avoid the adjustment costs that they may entail. Kelemen (2010), Kelemen and Vogel (2010), and Poletti and Sicurelli (2012, 2016), for instance, show how business groups, in some cases with the support of CSOs, have successfully pushed EU decision-makers to try to export costly regulatory standards in different international venues internationally both to avoid increased import penetration and to increase the export opportunities in foreign markets. Similarly, a recent study by

Lechner (2016) shows that lobbying triggered by import and wage pressures largely motivates the inclusion of social or environmental clauses in trade agreements.

2.5.2 *Domino Effects*

While sharing the view that policymakers respond to the preferences of organized business groups in the making of the trade policy, other scholars shed light on additional factors shaping such groups' pressures. This body of work focuses on the political dynamics engendered by the signing of PTAs and builds on the seminal work of Jacob Viner (1950) and the concepts of trade creation and trade diversion that he introduced in seeking to understand the distributive effects generated by such agreements. Trade agreements that eliminate/reduce tariffs against each other, while continuing to levy tariffs against imports from third countries, produce two effects. On the one hand, they create trade between PTA members, because some of the goods produced domestically may become uncompetitive with respect to those produced by other PTA members. On the other hand, they divert trade in that goods produced by a PTA member can become cheaper than those previously bought from outsiders.

Scholars increasingly rely on these important notions to explain the proliferation of PTAs that has characterized the international trade since the early 1990s, a pattern that is not likely to slow down in the near future (Dür et al. 2014). More specifically, countries' decisions to embark increasingly on these types of trade initiatives are accounted for by focusing on how trade diversion may motivate exporters in non-member countries to mobilize politically and ask their governments to neutralize such negative distributive effects by either joining PTAs or creating new ones. In addition to the general observation that policymakers tend to cater to the demands of organized business groups for either increased foreign market access opportunities or domestic protection from foreign competition, these scholars thus highlight that the trade policy choices may be driven by a domino effect triggered by the desire to offer 'protection for exporters' (Baldwin 1993). While exporters usually face greater collective action problems than import-competing groups when deciding to mobilize politically due to the high costs of information gathering about foreign market access opportunities, the greater uncertainty about the success of the lobbying effort, the uncertainty about who will capitalize on the increased market access opportunities, and the losses that they incur as a result of the trade diversion effects generate powerful incentives for mobilization and ultimately increase the political support for the signing of new trade agreements (Dür 2007a).

Dür (2007a, b, 2008) analyses various instances of EU trade negotiations to test empirically the so-called protection for exporters argument, that is, the proposition that exporters lobby more in reaction to losses of foreign market share than in pursuit of opportunities, including negotiations. Dür (2010) and Sbragia (2010) expand the argument further in a comparative analysis of US and EU trade policies over the last century, integrating domestic and international strategies into a single explanation to account for periods of acceleration and slowdown in the pace of trade liberalization in these political systems. Besides offering an outline of the 'protection for exporters' argument, Dür (2010) combines these insights with an explanation of bargaining outcomes when policies abroad harm a country's exporters. By relying on the concept of export vulnerability as a key factor in explaining the amount of concessions that one country is able to extract in the bargaining process, the explanation can account for why exporters in a given country exert pressure on decision-makers to seek increased access to foreign markets as well as the outcome of trade bargaining. In a recent quantitative analysis of the proliferation of PTAs among 167 countries, Baccini and Dür (2012) show that the explanatory force of the protection for exporters argument extends beyond the cases of two pivotal international trade players, such as the EU and the US.

2.5.3 *The Globalization of Production and the Emergence of GVCs*

While also conceiving of policymakers as political support maximizers who seek to avoid the mobilization of political enemies and whose ability to commit to trade liberalization ultimately depends on the relative balance of influence of those who favour and those who oppose the further opening of the economy to foreign products (Grossman and Helpman 1994, 2001; Magee et al. 1989; Schattsneider 1935), a third set of contributions complements the arguments reviewed so far by stressing how the globalization of production and the resulting emergence of global value chains (GVCs) have affected the politics of trade policy.

The globalization of trade, production, and distribution systems stands out as one of the most important developments in the contemporary international economy (Antràs 2010). Until the 1990s most retailers and producers in advanced capitalist economies bought or produced the bulk of their products and inputs domestically. However, the growth of the industrial capabilities of a number of important developing countries enabled such producers to cut their costs and streamline their production by outsourcing their labour-intensive, less value-added operations to low(er)-income countries while at the same time retaining core competencies, such as innovation and product strategy, marketing, and the highest value-added segments of manufacturing and services (Elms and Low 2013; Lanz and Miroudot 2011; OECD et al. 2013).

This process has been carried out through the creation of foreign subsidiaries—that is, by vertical FDI—or by relying on independent foreign suppliers (Lanz and Miroudot 2011). These altered (production) structures, which have become particularly common in labour-intensive consumer goods industries as well as the food industry, are usually referred to as GVCs (Burch and Lawrence 2005; Gereffi 1999). While the bulk of research based on the GVC framework focuses on conceptualizing and accounting for different inter-firm governance patterns *within* GVCs (Gereffi et al. 2005; Nadvi 2008), a growing number of works focus on the implications of these important changes for the making of trade policy. These studies show how GVCs gave rise to the political mobilization and empowerment of anti-protectionist societal interests and as such decreased the demands for protection during economic crises (Milner 1987), reduced the political support for the imposition of anti-dumping measures (Jensen et al. 2013, 2015), promoted support for trade liberalization through PTAs (Antràs and Staiger 2012; Baccini et al. 2014; Baldwin 2011; Chase 2003; Kim 2015; Manger 2009; Orefice and Rocha 2014), and increased the compliance with WTO rules (Yildirim et al. 2017).

The insights developed within this latter literature have found wide application in the study of EU trade policy. For instance, a growing body of work focuses on how these transnational chains of production have made the EU trade policy increasingly responsive to the preference, patterns of political mobilization, and influence of import-dependent firms, that is, firms and sectors that rely on income generated from the import of intermediate products for their production process. The argument here is that, because the EU is highly integrated into GVCs, many domestic firms rely on income generated by imports of intermediate products and welcome traditional exchanges of market access concessions, because they can lower the cost of imported inputs (Lanz and Miroudot 2011). Whether sourcing firms operate directly in a foreign country or simply import intermediate inputs from foreign suppliers is quite unimportant (Manger 2012). Moreover, as a result of mergers and acquisitions and vertical integration, import-dependent firms have undergone a dramatic move towards consolidation in the last decade and a half, increasing their capacity to mobilize politically (Eckhardt and Poletti 2016). These processes overall make trade liberalization easier to achieve politically.

These works examine the implications of GVCs for the EU trade defence instrument in general (Eckhardt 2013; De Bièvre and Eckardt 2011) and towards Asian countries (Eckhardt 2011, 2015), the EU bilateral trade strategies towards Asian countries (Eckhardt and Poletti 2016), and the EU responses in WTO disputes (Yildirim 2016). Recent analyses also focus on the implications of GVCs for understanding the politics of the TTIP negotiations in the EU, focusing in particular on how they incentivize economic actors to maximize their efficiency gains through the effective management of the trade–investment–service nexus (Baldwin 2014). According to De Bièvre and Poletti (2016) and Young (2016), the reason why the TTIP aroused relatively little opposition from business across the Atlantic is to be found in the fact that transatlantic business alliances rooted precisely in the interpenetration of the transatlantic economy driven by extensive cross-investments.

References

Antràs, P. 2010. *International Trade and Organizations.* National Bureau of Economic Research Report No. 2.

Antràs, P., and R.W. Staiger. 2012. Trade Agreements and the Nature of Price Determination. *The American Economic Review* 10 (3): 470–476.

Baccini, L., and A. Dür. 2012. The New Regionalism and Policy Interdependence. *British Journal of Political Science* 42 (1): 57–79.

Baccini L., A. Dür, and M. Elsig. 2014. *Global Supply Chains and the Political Economy of Preferential Tariff Liberalization.* Paper presented at the General Conference of the ECPR, Glasgow, September.

Baldwin, R. 1993. *A Domino Theory of Regionalism.* National Bureau of Economic Research, Working Paper No. 4465.

Baldwin, M. 2006. EU Trade Politics: Heaven or Hell? *Journal of European Public Policy* 13 (6): 926–942.

Baldwin, R. 2011. *Trade and Industrialisation After Globalisation's 2nd Unbundling: How Building and Joining a Supply Chain Are Different and Why It Matters.* Cambridge, MA: National Bureau of Economic Research.

———. 2014. WTO 2.0: Governance of 21st Century Trade. *The Review of International Organizations* 9 (2): 261–283.

Blustein, P. 2009. *Misadventures of the Most Favored Nations: Clashing Egos, Inflated Ambitions, and the Great Shambles of the World Trade System*. New York: Public Affairs.

Bohmer, A., and G. Glania. 2003. *The Doha Development Round: Reintegrating Business Interests into the Agenda*. Paper Series 'Beiträge zum internationalen Wirtschaftsrecht'. http://www.wirtschaftsrecht.uni-halle.de/sites/default/files/altbestand/Heft15.pdf.

Bossuyt, F. 2009. The Social Dimension of the New Generation of EU FTAs with Asia and Latin America: Ambitious Continuation for the Sake of Policy Coherence. *European Foreign Affairs Review 14* (5): 703–722.

Burch, D., and G. Lawrence. 2005. Supermarket Own Brands, Supply Chains and the Transformation of the Agri-Food System. *International Journal of Sociology of Agriculture and Food* 13 (1): 1–18.

Chase, K.A. 2003. Economic Interests and Regional Trading Arrangements: The Case of NAFTA. *International Organization* 57 (01): 137–174.

Conceição-Heldt, E., and S. Meunier. 2014. Speaking with a Single Voice. Internal Cohesiveness and External Effectiveness of the EU in World Politics. *Journal of European Public Policy* 21 (7): 961–979.

Croome, J. 1999. *Reshaping the World Trading System: a History of the Uruguay Round*. The Hague: Kluwer Law International.

De Bièvre, D. 2006. The EU Regulatory Trade Agenda and the Quest for WTO Enforcement. *Journal of European Public Policy* 13 (6): 851–866.

———. 2014. A Glass Quite Empty: Issue Groups' Influence in the Global Trade Regime. *Global Policy* 5 (2): 222–228.

De Bièvre, D., and A. Dür. 2005. Constituency Interests and Delegation in European and American Trade Policy. *Comparative Political Studies* 38 (10): 1271–1296.

De Bièvre, D., and J. Eckardt. 2011. Interest Groups and EU Anti-Dumping Policy. *Journal of European Public Policy* 18 (3): 339–360.

De Bièvre, D., and A. Poletti. 2016. Why the TTIP Is Not (So) New, and Why It Is Also Not (So) Bad. *Journal of European Public Policy*. https://doi.org/10.1080/13501763.2016.1254274

De Bièvre, D., A. Poletti, and L. Thomann. 2014. To Enforce or Not to Enforce? Judicialization, Venue Shopping and Global Regulatory Harmonization. *Regulation & Governance* 8 (3): 269–286.

De Bièvre, D., A. Poletti, M. Hanegraaff, and J. Beyers. 2016. International Institutions and Interest Mobilization. The WTO and Lobbying in EU and US Trade Policy. *Journal of World Trade* 50 (2): 289–312.

De Ville, F. 2016. *Regulatory Cooperation in TTIP: A Risk for Democratic Policy Making*. FEPS Policy Brief. Brussels: Foundation for European Progressive Studies.

De Ville, F., and G. Siles-Brügge. 2016. *TTIP: The Truth About the Transatlantic Trade and Investment Partnership*. Cambridge: Polity Press.

Deutsch, K.G. 2001. The EU: Contending for Leadership. In *The World Trade Organization Millennium Round. Freer Trade in the Twenty First Century*, ed. K.G. Deutsch and B. Speyer. London: Routledge.

Dür, A. 2007a. EU Trade Policy as Protection for Exporters: The Agreements with Mexico and Chile. *Journal of Common Market Studies* 45 (4): 833–855.

———. 2007b. Protection for Exporters: Foreign Discrimination and U.S. Trade Liberalization. *International Studies Quarterly* 51 (2): 457–480.

———. 2008. Bringing Economic Interests Back into the Study of EU Trade Policy-Making. *British Journal of Politics and International Relations* 10 (1): 27–45.

———. 2010. *Protection for Exporters: Power and Discrimination in Transatlantic Trade Relations, 1930–2010*. Ithaca: Cornell University Press.

Dür, A., and D. De Bièvre. 2007. Inclusion Without Influence: NGOs in European Trade Policy. *Journal of Public Policy* 27 (1): 79–101.

Dür, A., and L. Lechner. 2015. Business Interests and the Transatlantic Trade and Investment Partnership. In *The Politics of Transatlantic Trade Negotiations: TTIP in a Globalized World*, ed. J.F. Morin, T. Novotna, F. Ponjaert, and M. Telò, 69–79. Farnham: Ashgate.

Dür, A., and G. Mateo. 2014. Public Opinion and Interest Group Influence: How Citizen Groups Derailed the Anti-Counterfeiting Trade Agreement. *Journal of European Public Policy* 22 (8): 1199–1217.

Dür, A., L. Baccini, and M. Elsig. 2014. The Design of International Trade Agreements: Introducing a New Database. *Review of International Organizations* 9 (3): 353–375.

Eckhardt, J. 2011. Firm Lobbying and EU Trade Policy Making: Reflections on the Anti-Dumping Case Against Chinese and Vietnamese Shoes (2005–2011). *Journal of World Trade* 45 (5): 965–991.

———. 2013. EU Unilateral Trade Policy-Making: What Role for Import-Dependent Firms? *Journal of Common Market Studies* 51 (6): 989–1005.

———. 2015. *Business Lobbying and Trade Governance: The Case of EU-China Relations*. Basingstoke: Palgrave Macmillan.

Eckhardt, J., and A. Poletti. 2016. Trading with Asia: Import-Dependent Firms and EU-Asia Trade Agreements. *Journal of European Public Policy* 3 (10): 1543–1562.

Elms, D.K., and P. Low, eds. 2013. *Global Value Chains in a Changing World*. Geneva: World Trade Organization.

Elsig, M. 2007. The EU's Choice of Regulatory Venues for Trade Negotiations: A Tale of Agency Power. *Journal of Common Market Studies* 45 (4): 927–948.

European Commission. 1999. *Communication from the Commission to the Council and to the European Parliament: The EU Approach to the Millennium Round*. COM (99) 331 Final, 8 July.

———. 2006. Global Europe: Competing in the World. COM (2006) 567 final, October 4.

Falke, A. 2005. EU-USA Trade Relations in the Doha Development Round: Market Access Versus a Post-Modern Trade Policy Agenda. *European Foreign Affairs Review* 10: 339–357.

Feliu, L., and F. Serra. 2015. The European Union as a "Normative Power" and the Normative Voice of the European Parliament. In *The European Parliament and Its International Relations*, ed. S. Stavridis and D. Irrera, 17–34. London: Routledge.

Gereffi, G. 1999. International Trade and Industrial Upgrading in the Apparel Commodity Chain. *Journal of International Economics* 48 (1): 37–70.

Gereffi, G., J. Humphrey, and T. Sturgeon. 2005. The Governance of Global Value Chains. *Review of International Political Economy* 12 (1): 78–104.

Gowa, J., and S.Y. Kim. 2005. An Exclusive Country Club: The Effects of the GATT on Trade, 1950–94. *World Politics* 57 (4): 453–478.

Grossman, G.M., and E. Helpman. 1994. Protection for Sale. *The American Economic Review* 84 (4): 833–850.

———. 2001. *Special Interest Politics*. Cambridge, MA: MIT Press.

Heron, T., and G. Siles Brügge. 2012. Competitive Liberalization and the 'Global Europe' Services and Investment Agenda: Locating the Commercial Drivers of the EU–ACP Economic Partnership Agreements. *Journal of Common Market Studies* 50 (2): 250–266.

Hirsch, M. in press. Identity Matters: The Enforcement of Global Human Rights Treaties by European Union's Trade Instruments. In *International Economic Law and Human Rights*, ed. L. Biukovic and P. Edward Potter. Cheltenham: Edward Elgar Publishing.

Hiscox, M.J. 2001. Class versus Industry Cleavages: Inter-Industry Factor Mobility and the Politics of Trade. *International Organization* 55 (1): 1–46.

Holmes, P. 2006. Trade and "Domestic" Policies: The European Mix. *Journal of European Public Policy* 13 (6): 811–827.

Jensen, J.B., D.P. Quinn, and S. Weymouth. 2013. *Global Supply Chains, Currency Undervaluation, and Firm Protectionist Demands*. Cambridge, MA: National Bureau of Economic Research.

———. 2015. The Influence of Firm Global Supply Chains and Foreign Currency Undervaluations on US Trade Disputes. *International Organization* 69 (4): 913–947.

Jupille, J., W. Mattli, and D. Snidal. 2013. *Institutional Choice and Global Commerce*. Cambridge: Cambridge University Press.

Kelemen, D. 2010. Globalizing European Union Environmental Policy. *Journal of European Public Policy* 17 (3): 335–349.

Kelemen, D., and D. Vogel. 2010. Trading Places: The Role of the United States and the European Union in International Environmental Politics. *Comparative Political Studies* 43 (4): 427–456.

Khorana, S., and M. Garcia. 2013. *European Union–India Trade Negotiations: One Step Forward, One Back. Journal of Common Market Studies*. 51 (4): 684–700.

Kim, S.Y. 2015. Regionalization in Search of Regionalism: Production Networks and Deep Integration Commitments in Asia's PTAs. In *The Purpose, Design, and Effects of Preferential Trade Agreements*, ed. A. Dur and M. Elsig. Cambridge: Cambridge University Press.

Lanz, R., and S. Miroudot. 2011. *Intra-Firm Trade: Patterns, Determinants and Policy Implications*. Paris: OECD Publishing.

Larsén, M.F. 2007. Trade Negotiations Between the EU and South Africa: A Three-Level Game. *Journal of Common Market Studies* 45 (4): 857–881.

———. 2017. The Increasing Power of the European Parliament: Negotiating the EU-India Free Trade Agreement. *International Negotiation*. https://doi.org/10.1163/15718069-12341353.

Lechner, L. 2016. The Domestic Battle Over the Design of Non-Trade Issues in Preferential Trade Agreements. *Review of International Political Economy* 23 (5): 840–871.

Lucarelli, S. 2006. Introduction. Values, Principles, Identity and European Union Foreign Policy. In *Values and Principles in European Union Foreign Policy*, ed. S. Lucarelli and I. Manners, 1–18. London: Routledge.

Magee, S., W. Brock, and L. Young. 1989. *Black Hole Tariff and Endogenous Policy Theory*. Cambridge: Cambridge University Press.

Manger, M. 2009. *Investing in Protection: The Politics of Preferential Trade Agreements Between North and South*. Cambridge: Cambridge University Press.

———. 2012. Vertical Trade Specialization and the Formation of North-South PTAs. *World Politics* 64 (4): 622–658.

Manners, I. 2002. Normative Power Europe: A Contradiction in Terms? *Journal of Common Market Studies* 40 (2): 235–258.

Martin, L. 1992. Interests, Power, and Multilateralism. *International Organization* 46 (4): 765–792.

Meunier, S. 2003. Trade Policy and Political Legitimacy in the European Union. *Comparative European Politics* 1 (1): 67–90.

———. 2005. *Trading Voices: The European Union in International Commercial Negotiations*. Princeton, NJ: Princeton University Press.

———. 2007. Managing Globalization? The EU in International Trade Negotiations. *Journal of Common Market Studies* 45 (4): 905–926.

Meunier, S., and K. Nicolaïdis. 1999. Who Speaks for Europe? The Delegation of Trade Authority in the European Union. *Journal of Common Market Studies* 37 (3): 477–501.

———. 2006. The European Union as a Conflicted Trade Power. *Journal of European Public Policy* 13 (6): 906–925.

Milner, H. 1987. Resisting the Protectionist Temptation: Industry and the Making of Trade Policy in France and the United States During the 1970s. *International Organization* 41 (4): 639–665.

Nadvi, K. 2008. Global Standards, Global Governance, and the Organization of Global Value Chains. *Journal of Economic Geography* 8 (3): 323–343.

Nicolaïdis, K., and S. Meunier. 2002. Revisiting Trade Competence in the European Union: Amsterdam, Nice and Beyond. In *Institutional Challenges in the European Union*, ed. M. Hosli and A. van Deemen. London: Routledge.

OECD, UNCTAD, and WTO. 2013. Implications of Global Value Chains for Trade, Investment, Development and Jobs'. http://www.oecd.org/trade/G20-Global-Value-Chains-2013.pdf.

Orbie, J. 2011. Promoting Labour Standards Through Trade: Normative Power or Regulatory State Europe? In *Normative Power Europe*, ed. R.G. Whitman, 161–184. London: Palgrave Macmillan.

Orbie, J., and S. Khorana. 2015. Normative Versus Market Power Europe? The EU-India Trade Agreement. *Asia-Europe Journal* 13 (3): 253–264.

Orefice, G., and N. Rocha. 2014. Deep Integration and Production Networks: An Empirical Analysis. *The World Economy* 37 (1): 106–136.

Poletti, A. 2011. WTO Judicialisation and Preference Convergence in EU Trade Policy: Making the Agent's Life Easier. *Journal of European Public Policy* 18 (3): 361–382.

———. 2012. *The European Union and Multilateral Trade Governance: the Politics of the Doha Round*. London: Routledge.

———. 2013. Making Sense of Multiple Trade Politics: Explaining European Union Strategies in the Doha Round. *Italian Political Science Review* 43 (1): 97–124.

Poletti, A., and D. De Bièvre. 2014a. The Political Science of European Union Trade Policy: A Literature Review with a Research Outlook. *Comparative European Politics* 12 (1): 101–119.

———. 2014b. Political Mobilization, Veto Players, and WTO Litigation: Explaining European Union Responses in Trade Disputes. *Journal of European Public Policy* 21 (8): 1181–1198.

———. 2016. *Judicial Politics and International Cooperation: From Disputes to Deal-Making at the World Trade Organization*. Colchester: European Consortium for Political Research Press.

Poletti, A., and D. Sicurelli. 2012. The EU as a Promoter of Environmental Norms in the Doha Round. *West European Politics* 35 (4): 911–932.

———. 2016. The European Union, Preferential Trade Agreements, and the International Regulation of Sustainable Biofuels. *Journal of Common Market Studies* 54 (2): 249–266.

Poletti, A., D. Bièvre, and T. Chatagnier. 2015. Cooperation in the Shadow of WTO Law: Why Litigate When You Can Negotiate. *World Trade Review* 14 (S1): 33–58.

Pollack, M., and G. Shaffer. 2009. *When Cooperation Fails: The International Law and Politics of Genetically Modified Foods*. New York: Oxford University Press.

Riddervold, M. 2010. A Matter of Principle? EU Foreign Policy in the International Labour Organization. *Journal of European Public Policy* 17 (4): 581–598

Ripoll Servent, A. 2014. The Role of the European Parliament in International Negotiations After Lisbon. *Journal of European Public Policy* 21 (4): 568–586.

Rosamond, B. 2014. Three Ways of Speaking Europe to the World: Markets, Peace, Cosmopolitan Duty and the EU's Normative Power. *British Journal of Politics and International Relations* 16: 133–148.

Sbragia, A. 2010. The EU, the US, and Trade Policy: Competitive Interdependence in the Management of Globalization. *Journal of European Public Policy* 17 (3): 368–382.

Schattsneider, E. 1935. *Politics, Pressure and the Tariff.* New York: Prentice Hall.

Schott, J.J. 2000. *The WTO After Seattle.* Washington, DC: Institute for International Economics.

Sicurelli, D. 2016. The EU is a Normative Power in World Politics. In *Key Controversies in European Integration*, ed. H. Zimmermann and A. Dür, 192–198. London: Palgrave.

Siles-Brügge, G. 2014. *Constructing European Union Trade Policy: A Global Idea of Europe.* London: Palgrave Macmillan.

Sjursen, H., and G. Rosén. 2017. Arguing Sanctions. On the EU's Response to the Crisis in Ukraine. *Journal of Common Market Studies* 55 (1): 20–36.

Van den Hoven, A. 2002. *Interest Group Influence on Trade Policy in a Multilevel Polity: Analysing the EU Position at the Doha WTO Ministerial Conference.* EUI Working Papers 2002/67.

———. 2006. European Union Regulatory Capitalism and Multilateral Trade Negotiations. In *Values and Principles in European Foreign Policy*, ed. S. Lucarelli and I. Manners. London and New York: Routledge.

Van der Loo, G., and J. Pelkmans. 2016. *Does Wallonia's Veto of CETA Spell the Beginning of the End of EU Trade Policy?* CEPS Commentary, 26 October.

Viner, J. 1950. *The Customs Union Issue.* New York: Carnegie Endowment for International Peace.

Whitman, R. G. 2011. Norms, Power and Europe: A New Agenda for Study of the EU and International Relations. In *Normative Power Europe: Empirical and Theoretical Perspectives*, ed. by R. G. Whitman, 1–22. Hampshire: Palgrave Macmillan.

Woolcock, S. 2000. European Union Trade Policy: Global Pressures and Domestic Constraints. In *Policy Making in the European Union*, ed. H. Wallace and W. Wallace. Oxford: Oxford University Press.

———. 2005. Trade Policy: From Uruguay to Doha and Beyond. In *Policy-Making in the European Union*, ed. H. Wallace, W. Wallace, and M. Pollack. Oxford: Oxford University Press.

———. 2010a. Trade Policy: A Further Shift Towards Brussels. In *Policy-Making in the European Union*, ed. H. Wallace, M.A. Pollack, and A.R. Young, 381–398. Oxford: Oxford University Press.

———. 2010b. *The Treaty of Lisbon and the European Union as an Actor in International Trade.* ECIPE Working Paper, No. 1/2010, Brussels: European Centre for International Political Economy.

WTO. 2001. *Ministerial Declaration.* WT/MIN(01)/DEC/1, Doha, 20 November.

Yildirim, A. 2016. Domestic Political Implications of Global Value Chains: Explaining EU Responses to Litigation at the World Trade Organisation *Comparative European Politics.* https://doi.org/10.1057/s41295-016-0085-3.

Yildirim, A., T. Chatagnier, A. Poletti, and D. De Bièvre. 2017. The Internationalization of Production and the Politics of Compliance in WTO Disputes. *The Review of International Organizations.* https://doi.org/10.1007/s11558-017-9278-z.

Young, A. 2000. The Adaptation of European Foreign Economic Policy: From Rome to Seattle. *Journal of Common Market Studies* 38 (1): 93–116.

———. 2004. The Incidental Fortress: The Single Market and World Trade. *Journal of Common Market Studies* 2 (2): 393–414.

———. 2007. Trade Politics Ain't What It Used to Be: The European Union in the Doha Round. *Journal of Common Market Studies* 45 (4): 789–811.

———. 2016. Not Your Parents' Trade Conflict: The Transatlantic Trade and Investment Partnership Negotiations. *Review of International Political Economy* 23 (3): 345–378.

Young, A., and J. Peterson. 2006. The EU and the New Trade Politics. *Journal of European Public Policy* 13 (6): 795–814.

———. 2014. *Parochial Global Europe: 21st Century Trade Politics.* Oxford: Oxford University Press.

Young, A., P. Holmes, and J. Rollo. 2000. *The European Trade Agenda after Seattle.* SEI Working Paper No. 37. Brighton: Sussex European Institute.

CHAPTER 3

Trade Agreements with Latin American Countries

Abstract The EU has concluded comprehensive preferential trade agreements with Central American (CA) countries and the Andean Community (AC). Despite significant asymmetries in terms of the timing of the respective commitments, these agreements include provisions that significantly eliminate and/or reduce both tariff and non-tariff barriers to trade and promote stringent norms concerning human rights. Even though these trade partner countries have a relatively small market size, these agreements mobilized few but important exporting interests in the EU. More specifically, European producers and investors supported these trade deals with a view to level the playing field with their US counterparts, which had increased market access to these sets of countries thanks to the trade agreements signed with the US a few years earlier. Due to the low levels of integration of both CA countries and the AC, the political role of EU import-dependent firms remained marginal throughout these negotiations. While European farmers voiced their strong opposition to the prospect of an EU–MERCOSUR (Mercado Común del Sur) trade agreement, they did not mobilize to oppose EU trade agreements with these other Latin American countries. Opposition to these agreements mainly materialized in the form of concerns raised by some NGOs and trade unions over the human rights, environmental and labour rights implications of these agreements. However, the inclusion of a wide set of provisions dealing with these issues in the negotiating position of the EU was successful in diffusing this opposition over time.

A. Poletti, D. Sicurelli, *The Political Economy of Normative Trade Power Europe*, https://doi.org/10.1007/978-3-319-78864-7_3

Keywords Central America • Andean Community • domino effect • European exporters • civil society organizations

3.1 Introduction

The EU signed an Association Agreement with Central America (CA) on 29 June 2012. The part of the agreement that covers trade issues has been provisionally applied as from August 2013 with Nicaragua, Honduras, and Panama, as from October 2013 with El Salvador and Costa Rica, and finally as from December 2013 with Guatemala. At the same time, the EU signed a comprehensive trade agreement with Peru and Colombia in 2012, which has been provisionally applied since March and August 2013, respectively. In this case, the EU had started to negotiate a trade deal with the Andean Community (AC), which was a deal also comprising Ecuador and Bolivia. However, in the course of negotiations these two countries backtracked. After the agreement with Colombia and Peru was completed, Ecuador reassessed its position and resumed negotiations in 2014. The EU, together with Colombia and Peru, signed a protocol of accession with Ecuador, and in 2017 Ecuador finally joined the trade agreement. In addition to earlier bilateral trade agreements signed with Mexico in 1997 and Chile in 2002, these two sets of trade relations represent the core of EU trade relations with Latin American countries.[1]

The rationale for the EU's decision to negotiate trade agreements with these countries is largely to be found in the political-economy factors that affect the politics of trade in the EU. More specifically, this chapter shows that, despite the relatively minor importance of both CA and the Andean group as trading partners for the EU, these trade agreements serve the purposes of furthering the interests of exporters in the machinery, transport equipment, and chemicals sectors while counterbalancing the US activist trade policy and the resulting potential negative effects of the trade agreements the US had signed a few years earlier with both groups of countries. In the context of both sets of trade relations, moreover, import-competing groups met these trade initiatives with little resistance. Indeed, all these countries already benefit from zero tariffs on almost all exports to the EU under the extended GSP-plus, which means that only a few sectors will enjoy enhanced access to this market. Opposition to these agreements has come in the form of the mobilization of a few CSOs in the EU voicing concerns about the implications of these agreements' for human and labour rights, environmental sustainability, and biodiversity.

The chapter is structured as follows. Sections 3.2 and 3.3 outline the content of the two agreements, sporadically referring to trade agreements signed by these countries with the US to highlight similarities and differences between the EU trade strategy and the strategy pursued by the US. Section 3.4 focuses on the political processes underlying the EU negotiating positions and the final outcomes of such negotiations. It analyses the demands and political pressures exerted on EU policymakers by key groups representing European business interests and CSOs. The conclusions discuss the broader implications of these trade agreements for the debate on the nature of the EU trade policy strategy.

3.2 The EU–CA Trade Agreement

The trade chapter of the Association Agreement signed on 29 June 2012 governs trade relations between the EU and CA countries, that is, Guatemala, Honduras, Nicaragua, Costa Rica, El Salvador, and Panama. The trade chapter is therefore one of three complementary pillars—political dialogue, cooperation, and trade—upon which the EU strategy with this set of countries rests in order to support economic growth, democracy, and political stability. The agreement is presented as the first example of the conclusion of a region-to-region agreement to be successfully negotiated by the EU, and it is also meant to set a precedent for further 'new generation' trade agreements with South American countries, including the now revitalized negotiations with the MERCOSUR (Woolcock et al. 2012).

The specifics of the trade liberalization commitments show that the EU has respected the self-declared goal of addressing the development needs of CA countries, particularly with regard to the timing of the respective tariff elimination commitments. For instance, commitments concerning agricultural trade require CA countries to phase out tariffs on most EU exports in ten years, with the exclusion of a number of important sensitive sectors (e.g. beef, pork, sugar, and rice), while the EU mostly grants duty-free access to its market immediately, with few exceptions, envisaging a longer phase-out period of seven years and the exclusion of certain sensitive sectors.

Similar asymmetries characterize the timing of trade liberalization commitments concerning manufactured goods. While CA countries committed to generally granting duty-free access to EU products within 10 years, and for only 4% of products after 15 years, the EU offered secure duty-free entry for all products immediately (European Commission 2011). It is important to note that because most CA exports to the EU already benefit from duty-free access to the EU under the GSP-plus scheme, the expected gains for CA countries concentrate on those products that still faced duties at the time of entry into force of the agreement, most notably sugar, bananas, and frozen shrimps. Despite these relatively limited distributive effects, the agreement is important insofar as it provides legally secure access to the EU market, avoiding the possibility that a future reform of the GSP-plus scheme could result in some CA countries graduating out of the scheme as middle-income countries.

With regard to rules of origin, the agreement contains comprehensive provisions aimed at strengthening inter-regional trade by allowing bilateral cumulation, that is, cumulation with material originating from CA countries, and diagonal cumulation, in other words, cumulation with respect to materials originating in countries with which the EU has trade agreements in regions such as Colombia, Ecuador, Peru, and Mexico.

On services, the agreement goes significantly beyond commitments undertaken in the WTO and secures wide access to many services, meeting the EU's key interests in the telecommunication, environmental, financial, and maritime services (European Commission 2011). The deal, however, also establishes that nothing in the agreement requires the privatization of public undertakings or public utilities services supply in the exercise of governmental authority, or the right to introduce new regulations to meet legitimate national policy objectives in the service sector. Moreover, the agreement allows for the exclusion of some sensitive sectors from the liberalization commitments, most notably the financial service sector.

On the SPS and TBT, the agreement is consistent with the WTO while including a number of WTO-plus measures by providing for bilateral and regional consultations on SPS-related measures in specific committees and by offering special and differential treatment in order to avoid unnecessary obstacles to CA exports in the EU.

As for the protection of IPR, the agreement reaffirms the parties' commitments to the TRIPS Agreement and the Convention on Biodiversity, adding a few general provisions to ensure that these general commitments can be effectively enforced. Most importantly, the agreement includes TRIPS-plus protection in the form of an extensive register of regional specialities, so-called geographical indications, following the EU approach.

As a result, over 200 geographical indications will be protected in the CA markets, while 10 are recognized in the EU market.

The agreement also includes provisions on public procurement, opening a wide range of public procurement to firms from any of the states that are parties to the agreement, which will be treated equally as domestic firms. The scale of the EU government procurement market is greater than that offered by CA countries, while the opening of CA countries' public procurement markets varies in terms of levels of liberalization, with Costa Rica and Panama opening their markets more significantly than other partners (Woolcock et al. 2012). The agreement also calls for national governments to ban all types of anti-competitive practices. Yet, the agreement also explicitly allows a party to maintain monopolies and state enterprises when these exist in accordance with domestic legislation.

Finally, the agreement includes binding provisions on human rights. Respect for democratic principles and fundamental human rights, as laid down in the Universal Declaration of Human Rights, is declared to constitute essential elements of the agreement, although the agreement does not foresee the creation of specific mechanisms dedicated to monitoring and implementing the human rights clause. The agreement supplements the essential elements clause, with a non-execution clause permitting the adoption of appropriate measures if one of the two parties violates the clause.

With respect to sustainable development, the agreement reiterates the promotion of core international conventions concerning labour rights and environmental protection that were already included in the GSP-plus scheme as conditionality measures with those countries. The agreement also established a joint Trade and Sustainable Development Board to effectively monitor and implement these sustainable development obligations. In contrast to the EU–Korea FTA, concluded in 2009, though, the composition of the domestic advisory group established by the Trade and Sustainable Development Board in the trade agreement with CA is not defined (Orbie et al. 2017).

3.3 The EU–AC Trade Agreement

As in the case of negotiations with CA countries, the EU initially wished to negotiate with the so-called AC countries on a region-to-region basis. Despite these initial ambitions, it soon became clear that such an outcome was infeasible, mostly due to the opposition of Bolivia and Ecuador to the EU positions on key aspects of discussions concerning IPR protection (Garcia 2015). Ecuador reconsidered its position against the trade agreement with the EU. In December 2013, the EU had announced that Ecuador no longer fulfilled the eligibility criteria to enjoy the GSP benefits, which would be removed as from 1 January 2015. Following this decision, Ecuador decided to resume negotiations with the EU, a decision that ultimately led to the signing of a protocol of accession, which entered into force in 2017.

The contents of the agreements signed by the EU with Colombia, Peru, and Ecuador are largely similar to those between the EU and CA countries outlined in the previous sections (see Table 3.1). Although the EU has signed a specific trade agreement with each of these three countries, many of the issues are largely identical across these agreements. We therefore do not discuss each and every aspect of these agreements separately, but provide an outline of the commitments undertaken between the EU and these countries as a whole, stressing important differences that may exist between them whenever necessary.

As discussed previously in the case of EU–CA negotiations, the EU sensitivity to the development needs of the AC countries mostly takes the shape of asymmetrical reciprocity with respect to the timing of the trade liberalization commitments. Commitments concerning the liberalization of agricultural trade, for instance, require AC countries to provide duty-free access on 85% of EU agricultural exports in 17 years, while for a subset of goods the agreement envisages the reduction of important non-tariff barriers such as alcohol monopolies and tax discrimination. As for increasing access to the EU market, many agricultural products originating from AC countries have already benefited from duty-free access under the GSP-plus scheme. Agricultural products benefiting from an improvement in market access are therefore limited and comprise mostly bananas, fresh table grapes, and fresh shrimps. For some of these products, duty-free access is granted upon entry into force of the agreements, for others after a transitional period of 11 years, while for goods that are not fully liberalized the agreement provides for increases in quota allowances and for reductions in tariffs.

Again, similar asymmetries characterize the timing of liberalization commitments concerning manufactured goods. AC countries committed to phasing out tariffs on imports of EU industrial goods in a period ranging from 6 to 11 years, while the EU has already granted duty-free access to most imports of manufactured goods from AC countries under the GSP-plus scheme. As in the case of CA countries, the implications of the agreement are nonetheless to be considered important given that the agreement ensures the continuation of these market access commitments even in the face of a reform of the GSP-plus scheme. With respect to rules of origin, again as in the case of EU–CA trade relations, the agreement allows for bilateral and diagonal cumulation, and therefore cumulation with respect to materials originating from CA countries, Southern American or Caribbean countries, or other countries that have signed a preferential agreement with the EU. Similarities with the EU–CA agreement can also be detected with respect to services. In this area too, the agreement goes significantly beyond commitments undertaken in the WTO and secures wide access to many EU service providers, meeting the EU's key interests in the telecommunication, environmental, professional, and maritime transport services (European Commission 2012). Yet, the agreement also identifies significant exceptions, which forecloses access to AC countries service markets in sensitive sectors such as mining, energy, research, and security services.

On the SPS and TBT standards, the agreement is consistent with the WTO while including a number of WTO-plus measures. These include guidelines for conducting verifications, schedules for reporting and consultation, specific rules on import administration, disciplines on labelling, and greater cooperation on technical regulations, standards, and conformity assessment by providing for bilateral and regional consultations on SPS-related measures in specific committees and by offering special and differential treatment in order to avoid unnecessary obstacles to CA exports in the EU.

As for the protection of IPR, the agreement largely overlaps with the EU–CA countries' agreement by reaffirming the parties' commitments to the TRIPS Agreement and the Convention on Biodiversity, and including TRIPS-plus protection in the form of an extensive register of 'geographical indications', which results in over 100 EU geographical indications being protected in the AC countries' markets. These agreements are partly different, however, in that they specify the need to ensure that IPR are supportive and do not run against the rights of indigenous people and local communities.

The agreement also includes provisions on public procurement, which significantly serves EU interests for two reasons. First, its rules on transparency and non-discrimination in public procurement have been substantially copy-pasted from the Revised Government Procurement Agreement (GPA), even though AC countries had not been signatories to such a plurilateral agreement signed under the auspices of the WTO (Araujo 2016). Second, they entail a commitment from AC countries to provide full access to the procurement of local municipalities, in addition to that of central authorities. The agreement also provides for the liberalization of investments in the form of market access via establishment and provision of national treatment, although it does not cover investment protection, given that it was negotiated before the formal extension of exclusive EU competence to foreign direct investments in the Treaty of Lisbon. The rules on investment are mainly located in the services chapter of the agreements and are in line with the GATS obligations (Wu 2012).

Finally, the provisions of the EU–AC countries' trade agreements on competition, human rights, and sustainable development are largely identical to those of the EU–CA trade agreement. This agreement also calls for national governments to ban anti-competitive practices, while explicitly allowing parties to maintain monopolies and state enterprises when these exist in accordance with domestic legislation. These agreements also explicitly call for the respect of democratic principles and fundamental human rights, as laid down in the Universal Declaration of Human Rights, while not foreseeing the creation of specific mechanisms dedicated to monitoring and implementing the human rights clause. And to conclude, these agreements equally include provisions concerning sustainable development that entail obligations to respect and effectively implement the fundamental ILO conventions and a number of multilateral environmental agreements, commitments that are to be monitored and effectively implemented through the creation of a joint Trade and Sustainable Development subcommittee. As in the agreement with CA, commitments on sustainable development included in the EU–Peru–Colombia agreement are rather conservative and flexible. Articles on civil society involvement, for instance, leave much discretion to the parties. The agreement has also attracted criticism for the lack of transparency in the procedure for selecting CSOs called to participate in the monitoring of the agreement (Orbie et al. 2017).

Table 3.1 The EU–CA and EU–AC trade agreements

	EU–CA	*EU–AC*
Market access to the EU	Duty-free access immediately or within 7 years	Duty-free access immediately or within 11 years
Market access to the partner	Duty-free access mostly within 10 and in some cases 15 years	Duty-free access within 6, 11, or 17 years
Anti-dumping	No infant industry protection clause Standard reciprocal bilateral safeguard measures to protect domestic producers	No infant industry protection clause Standard reciprocal bilateral safeguard measures to protect domestic producers
Rules of origin	Bilateral and diagonal cumulation	Bilateral and diagonal cumulation
Trade in service	WTO-plus liberalization of telecommunication, financial, environmental, and maritime transport sectors	WTO-plus liberalization of telecommunication, professional, environmental and maritime transport sectors Exceptions for sensitive markets: mining, energy, research, and security services
Government procurement	Framework rules in public procurement Liberalization varies by country	Extend transparency provisions of GPA to CA Liberalization of local municipalities' government procurement markets
Intellectual property rights	TRIPS-consistent protection plus 200 EU geographical indications	TRIPS-plus protection plus 100 EU geographical indications
Sustainable development	Calling for ratification and enforcement of all the core UN environmental and labour conventions Establishment of a joint Trade and Sustainability Board to monitor and implement obligations	Calling for ratification and enforcement of all the core UN environmental and labour conventions Establishment of a joint Trade and Sustainability Board to monitor and implement obligations
Human rights	Respect for democratic principles and fundamental human rights as laid down in the Universal Declaration of Human Rights	Respect for democratic principles and fundamental human rights as laid down in the Universal Declaration of Human Rights

3.4 Tracing Preferences in Negotiations with Latin American Countries

The EU decision to start negotiations and then sign trade agreements with both CA and the AC countries seems at first glance difficult to explain on the basis of explanations centred on economic rationales. Indeed, for the EU, both sets of countries are quite marginal from an economic viewpoint. The CA countries together account for only 0.3% of total EU exports, placing them outside the category of the top 40 EU markets. Peru, Colombia, and Ecuador considered together double this figure, making 0.2%, 0.3%, and 0.1% of total EU exports, respectively (European Commission 2016). The opposite is not true. The EU is a crucial trading partner for both trading blocks, ranking second as a trading partner for these countries, after the US, which remains by far the country with which these countries have the most important trading relationship. These figures show quite clearly that while both CA and AC countries may have had an interest in furthering trade relations with the EU, the economic stakes in these negotiations were quite marginal for the EU, which has led some analysts to question whether these agreements are good for the policy of negotiating with significant markets embodied in the 2006 Global Europe strategy (Woolcock et al. 2012; Stevens et al. 2012). As we argue in detail in the remainder of this section, however, these figures should not obscure the fact that important political-economy dynamics were at play in the politics underlying the EU trade strategy with these countries. First, the decision to embark on these negotiations can be explained by a domino effect triggered by the US decision to sign trade agreements with both sets of countries a few years earlier. The US had promoted negotiations for the signing of an FTA with the Dominican Republic and CA countries in 2003, also known as CAFTA-DR, which finally entered into force in 2009 when all countries ratified it. Similarly, the US began negotiations with Peru, Colombia, and Ecuador in 2004, which were completed in 2006, with the exception of Ecuador, which decided to backtrack from these negotiations during the process (Schott 2006). The agreement with Peru was ratified in 2009, and the agreement with Colombia in 2011. As Dür (2007) notes in his analysis of EU trade agreements with Mexico and Chile, from a political-economy perspective even losses that on aggregate appear small can have major political consequences if they are concentrated on relatively few players, giving them incentives to mobilize politically. Therefore, although neither group of countries are economically pivotal for the EU, the incentives brought about by the US trade strategy to avoid losses of market shares for EU firms exporting to these countries played a major role in shaping the EU trade strategy towards these countries (Fritz 2010; Dominiguez 2015). As Garcia (2015, p. 633) nicely puts it, 'in this climate EU leaders agreed to begin negotiations with CA and the AC [...]. The EU leaders placed economic interests, or rather potential future economic interests, first'.

Second, both groups of countries already benefited from duty-free access to the EU market under the GSP-plus scheme. This means that the costs in terms of increased import penetration from these trading partners could be expected to be quite small and limited to a few sectors. For this reason, the political pressures of those exporters standing to gain from increased access to these foreign markets was met with little resistance from EU producers, which created a favourable political environment for the European Commission to negotiate and conclude these trade agreements. For instance, while COPA-COGECA (Committee of Professional Agricultural Organizations—General Committee for Agricultural Cooperation in the European Union), the organization representing European farmers' interests, voiced its strong opposition to the prospect of an EU–MERCOSUR trade agreement (Garcia 2015), it did not mobilize to oppose EU trade agreements with these other Latin American countries. Opposition to these trade agreements thus came mostly in the form of concerns expressed by a few CSOs regarding their implications for human rights and sustainable development. However, the relatively far-reaching provisions on these issues included in the agreements allowed the European Commission to overcome this opposition and successfully conclude negotiations.

Finally, negotiations only marginally mobilized import-dependent groups such as retailer associations. The AC and CA countries, as a matter of fact, are not highly integrated in the GVCs. They mainly export raw materials (agricultural products, foodstuffs, beverages and tobacco, animal or vegetable fats and oils) or semi-transformed goods with little added value, which makes them less attractive than ASEAN markets (see Chap. 5) for import-dependent interest groups (Table 3.2).

3.4.1 *Market Access and Trade in Services*

The balance of business opinions in the EU was strongly in favour of both negotiations and ratification of EU trade agreements with CA countries and the AC, with a particular emphasis on how these trade strategies might bring about significant benefits for EU firms, both traditional exporters and service providers. All relevant organizations representing business interests in the EU have consistently supported these trade agreements in various ways. For instance, BusinessEurope made its voice heard on different occasions supporting the trade agreement and praising its positive effects for EU exporters. The EU–Colombia and Peru trade agreements were seen positively in that they secured access to these two important export markets in agricultural products and processed agricultural products, and because they envisaged 100% coverage of industrial products within ten years (Business Europe 2012). Similarly, BusinessEurope (Eurochambres and BusinessEurope 2012) expressed support for trade agreements with both the AC and CA countries in view of the significant gains they could bring about for telecommunication, construction, distribution, financial and transport services, as well as for the textiles, chemicals, wine, and spirits sectors.

More specifically on services, BusinessEurope underscored that the services chapter of the agreement is very ambitious, surpassing by far the levels of legally binding commitments undertaken in the GATS and therefore effectively offering new market access to European companies in a majority of sectors (BusinessEurope 2012). For these reasons, BusinessEurope forcefully asked members of the European Parliament to approve both sets of trade agreements. Those pressures for a WTO-plus agreement found support in the European Commission. A DG trade official claimed that they were consistent with its negotiating mandate, stressing that 'if you do not reach a deal on WTO-plus issues, then you do not need to have an agreement'.[2] The EU trade strategy towards these Latin American countries was also strongly supported by the European Services Forum, the umbrella organization representing the interests of European service providers. In contrast to arguments highlighting the small size of the countries' markets, the European Services Forum emphasized that 'the Colombian, Peruvian and Central American markets are often falsely assumed to be only very modest in size; this is however a dangerous misperception, for the combined population of the eight countries included in the agreement is 118 million [...] there is therefore a large potential market of consumers of middle-income level and with an impressive growth potential' (European Services Forum 2011, p. 1). Moreover, the association stressed the importance of these agreements for EU service interests in the telecommunication, environmental, financial, and maritime transport services, as well as their potential to lead to an increase of 25–30% in the trade flow value on both sides (European Services Forum 2012).

Quite interestingly, the agreement between the EU and the AC was also supported by Eurocommerce, the European association representing the interests of import-dependent firms, which encouraged the lifting of existing tariff and non-tariff barriers for imports and exports and the liberalization of trade in services (Eurocommerce 2007).

A number of factors suggest that the competition with the US in these markets, a competition made more severe by the successful US strategy of trade liberalization via FTAs, was a key factor driving both business and the European Commission support for this particular trade strategy. As already mentioned above, the timing of the negotiations, signings, and ratifications of these agreements show that the US preceded the EU in engaging with a strategy of trade liberalization with these sets of countries at bilateral and regional levels. The 2006 Global Europe strategy had already underlined that the criteria that would guide the choice of new partners for trade agreements included market potential, the level of protection against EU export interests, but also potential partners' negotiations with EU competitors (European Commission 2006). Unsurprisingly, when arguing in favour of strengthening the strategic partnership with Latin American countries, the European Commission stressed that, despite Europe being a leading foreign investor in the region, the US and Asia were gaining ground (European Commission 2006). Interestingly, European business clearly motivated its support for these agreements by pointing to the potential negative repercussions of the US trade strategy in the region. The European Services Forum (2011, p. 1), for instance, called on members of the European Parliament to approve these agreements by arguing that 'the European Parliament must be mindful of the competitive disadvantage it would face should the EU's own FTAs not be consented to'.

In addition to the timing of these negotiations and the self-declared motivations of both public officials and business groups, the content of the agreements also clearly supports the argument that competition with the US in these markets was an important factor. Woolcock et al. (2012) conducted a comprehensive comparison of the content of the agreements signed between the EU and the US with CA countries and showed with great clarity that on market access and service trade, the EU agreement ensures a level playing field with the US. The commitments of the two agreements concerning the liberalization of manufactured goods are almost identical, with both agreements requiring CA countries to offer duty-free access within 10 years for most products and 15 years for all products, while minor differences exist with regard to agricultural trade whereby the EU obtained even more generous concessions than the US. As for the service sector, the analysis shows that the commitments offered to the EU are at least as good as the ones offered in the US deal. Stevens et al. (2012) reached similar conclusions in their comparison of

EU and US trade agreements signed with the AC, showing that, despite small differences, EU exporters obtained equivalent access to Colombian and Peruvian markets as the US exporters.

3.4.2 *Public Procurement, Competition, and IPR*

The negotiating positions on public procurement and IPR have also been widely supported by business interests in the EU, both in light of their potential to open up new markets in CA and the AC and for their potential to protect European exporters from competition with their US counterparts. For instance, the European Services Forum (2011, 2012) praised the agreement with CA countries and the AC for their potential to open public procurement markets, particularly those of Panama and Costa Rica, and to promote rules on competition that would promote a level playing field. The European Services Forum (2011) also praised these agreements for their potential to strengthen economic competition and improve value, resulting in more internationally competitive economies. Similarly, BusinessEurope welcomed deals with CA countries and the AC because of their potential to reduce behind-the-border obstacles to trade and their potential to create a more favourable business environment (Business Europe 2012; Eurochambres and BusinessEurope 2012). In a joint declaration by a wide set of European business organizations, including BusinessEurope, the European Services Forum, the European Automobile Manufacturers' Association, and DigitalEurope, the agreements were praised because of their contribution to opening up public procurement markets and to promoting best practices for operators and investors (Joint Declaration 20212).

Similar statements of support characterize the debate on the provisions concerning IPR. For instance, Eurocommerce supported these agreements, highlighting their potential to foster the effective implementation of standards for IPR protection (Eurocommerce 2007). In the same vein, the European Services Forum (2011) stressed the importance of these agreements for their substantial commitments in IPR protection, including geographical indications, which are perceived to carry significant importance for European service companies.

In this case too, the positions of the main organizations representing European business interests should come as no surprise. Indeed, a comparison of the provisions of EU and US trade agreements with these sets of countries concerning these specific issue areas shows that the EU has been able to obtain similar treatment for European exporters to that for

US competitors and to even go beyond what was achieved by the US. As Woolcock et al. (2012) show, the EU trade agreement with CA countries opens public procurement markets to European companies to a larger extent than the US–CA countries' trade agreement does for US companies, offers comparable IPR protection while promoting TRIPS-plus protection of geographical indications not covered by the US–CA trade agreement, and finally includes similar levels of cooperation with respect to competition. Similarly, Stevens et al. (2012) comprehensively illustrate that the EU trade agreements with the AC also show how these agreements effectively contribute to responding to competitive pressures with the US. On public procurement, for instance, the EU was able to obtain greater access to these markets than the US by liberalizing public procurement of local municipalities, while on IPR protection and competition, the EU and US agreements are largely comparable (Colombian Ministry for Commerce, Industry and Tourism 2012), although in the former case the EU agreement goes a bit further by providing a very broad recognition of geographical indications. Interestingly, Stevens et al. (2012) also show that the EU trade agreements with CA countries and the AC served the purpose of levelling the playing field not only with the US but also with regard to China and Canada, two trading partners that had signed trade agreements with Colombia and Peru just before the EU.

3.4.3 Human Rights and Sustainable Development

The topics of human rights and sustainable development of these trade negotiations are the ones that raised most controversy in the EU. The long tradition of cooperation between European and Latin American CSOs made the negotiations with CA and the AC central in the agenda of European NGOs and trade unions.[3] The International Federation on Human Rights, FIDH (2012), and the European Trade Union Confederation (ETUC)[4] joined the International Office for Human Rights—Action on Colombia (OIDHACO 2010) in pushing for binding norms on human rights and labour rights in the agreement. According to the OIDHACO (2010), any agreement taking a soft stance on those issues would have been 'counterproductive and irresponsible'.

Fritz (2010) reports various arguments of NGOs opposing these agreements for their alleged negative impact on the sustainable growth opportunities of these countries, the weak mechanisms for monitoring human rights and labour rights violations, and these agreements' potential negative effects on environmentally sustainable production processes. As a result of these concerns, the European Parliament put forth a resolution asking Colombia and Peru to define a road map to guarantee the protection of labour rights, the environment, and human rights in the trade agreements ratification process (Euractiv 2012). After the conclusion of the negotiations, Oxfam and the OIDHACO produced a manifesto warning about the potential of these agreements to negatively affect existing inequalities between the EU and these countries, adding that their likely outcome would be to reduce development programmes and regional growth (Euractiv 2012). The Iniciativa de Copenhague para Centroamérica y México (CIFCA 2012) joined the criticism of the lack of binding enforcement mechanisms for the sustainable development chapter.

The ETUC sent a letter to the members of the European Parliament urging them not to support these agreements, pointing to the terrible human rights record in some of these countries and to the damage these agreements could bring about to the EU's reputation as a leading force in the promotion of human rights and basic freedoms (ETUC 2012). However, the ETUC was aware that European Parliament resolutions have no binding force on the European Commission and they and other European CSOs continued expressing their criticism against the sustainable chapters in the trade agreements with Latin American countries. After the conclusion of the two deals, they agreed to join the civil society mechanisms established to ensure that the sustainable development provisions of the agreement are effectively implemented. As declared by one development NGO, 'Look where we are standing now. … Before, we were shouting against the agreement on the streets; today, we are helping to implement it inside this building' (Orbie et al. 2017).

Business interests promoted a softer approach to sustainable development in the agreement. The European Services Forum (2011), for instance, considered the promotion of the international ILO convention as an instrument to increase average national wages for both skilled and unskilled workers. BusinessEurope (2012) also welcomed these agreements' provisions on labour and environmental protection as an effective means to ensure development and improved social protection in these Latin American countries. DG Trade shared those arguments and remarked that the sustainable development chapter in trade agreements with Latin American countries was more ambitious than those included in the US trade agreements, which only promoted minimum standards of labour and environmental protection without reference to international law.[5]

Table 3.2 Political-economy dynamics in the trade negotiations with CA countries and the AC

	Interest group mobilization for market access	*Domino effect*	*GVCs*
EU–CA negotiations	• Exporters (manufacturers and service providers) • NGOs	US–CAFTA-DR entered into force in 2009	Low integration
EU–AC	• Exporters (manufacturers and service providers) • NGOs	US trade negotiations with Colombia, Peru, and Ecuador started in 2004. Trade agreement with Peru ratified in 2009 and with Colombia in 2011	Low integration

3.5 Conclusion

The trade agreements negotiated and signed by the EU with CA countries and the AC entail relatively small economic stakes for the EU. This observation would seem to support the view that the EU was motivated by other than economic rationales in its trade strategy towards these sets of countries. However, a closer look at the content and political processes underlying these agreements reveals that the defence of the EU's economic interests was a key factor shaping the EU's strategy. Although the market size of these countries is certainly relatively small, these agreements significantly increase market access opportunities for a few important exporting sectors, a prospect that has generated consistent support for these agreements by all relevant organizations representing business interests in the EU. Securing access to these markets to key European manufacturers and service providers was made all the more important by the potential negative implications of the US trade strategies towards these countries. These agreements served the purpose of ensuring that the trade diversion effects of the trade agreements signed between the US and both groups of Latin American countries would not put European producers and investors at a disadvantage with respect to their US competitors. Therefore, this means that the EU trade strategy towards these sets of countries can be plausibly described as an attempt to defend key European economic interests by way of the creation of a level playing field with US business operators. The relatively small size of these countries' economies made this strategy relatively easy to achieve politically. As our analysis shows, we could not detect any opposition to the prospect of these agreements from business groups in the EU. Opposition to these agreements did materialize in the form of concerns raised by some CSOs over the human rights, environmental and labour rights implications of these agreements. However, the existence of a wide set of provisions dealing with these issues in the agreements diffused this opposition over time.

Notes

1. The EU has also formalized trade relations with the Caribbean in the framework of EU–ACP cooperation, while trade negotiations with the Mercado Común del Sur (MERCOSUR) have been ongoing for years but are nowhere near completion.
2. Interview, DG Trade, 16 July 2014.
3. Interview, ETUC, Brussels, 19 July 2017.
4. Interview, ETUC, Brussels, 19 July 2017.
5. Interview, DG Trade, Brussels, 6 June 2014.

References

Araujo, M.B.A. 2016. *The EU Deep Trade Agenda. Law and Policy*. Oxford: Oxford University Press.

BusinessEurope. 2012. *Speaking Points for Adrian Van den Hoven, Director for International Relations, EU Colombia and Peru Trade Agreement—European Parliament Hearing*. Brussels, 29 February.

Colombian Ministry for Commerce, Industry and Tourism. 2012. Colombia-European Union Partnership Agreement. Virtual Interview with Mister of Trade, Industry and Tourism, Sergio Diaz-Granados, 26 June.

Dominiguez, R. 2015. *EU Foreign Policy Towards Latin America*. Basingstoke: Palgrave Macmillan.

Dür, A. 2007. EU Trade Policy as Protection for Exporters: The Agreements with Mexico and Chile. *Journal of Common Market Studies* 45 (4): 833–855.

ETUC. 2012. *Letter to the Members of the European Parliament on the Proposed Free Trade Agreement with Colombia and Peru*. Brussels, 22 February.

Euractiv. 2012. *EU Latin America Trade Deals in Troubled Water*. Brussels, 28 June.

Eurochambres and Business Europe. 2012. *Future Trade Deals with Colombia/Peru and Central America to Boost EU Business*. Press Release, Brussels, 27 June.

Eurocommerce. 2007. *Free Trade Negotiations EU-Andean Community: Contribution to the DG Trade Stakeholder Consultation. Position* Paper, Brussels, 31 May.

European Commission. 2006. *A Stronger Partnership Between the European Union and Latin America*. Brussels. http://eeas.europa.eu/la/docs/com05_636_en.pdf.

———. 2011. *Highlights of the Trade Pillar of the Association Agreement Between Central America and the European Union*. Brussels, 20 June. http://europa.eu/rapid/press-release_MEMO-11-429_en.htm.

———. 2012. *Highlights of the Trade Agreement Between Colombia, Peru and the European Union*. Brussels, 26 June. http://europa.eu/rapid/press-release_MEMO-12-487_en.htm?locale=en.

———. 2016. European Union: Trade in Goods with Central America. http://trade.ec.europa.eu/doclib/docs/2006/september/tradoc_113478.pdf.

European Services Forum. 2011. *Services Industry Calls the European Parliament to Give Its Consent for the Conclusion of the EU-Colombia, Peru and Central American FTAs*. Letter to the Chairman of the International Trade Committee of the European Parliament, ESF11-16, Brussels, 21 November.

———. 2012. *The Voice of European Services Sectors in International Trade: EU-Central America*. 11 December. http://www.esf.be/new/esf-eu-trade-policy/eu-free-trade-agreements/eu-central-america/.

FIDH. 2012. FTA: The Colombian Road Map Does Not Respect EP Conditions. Press Release, 9 November.

Fritz, T. 2010. *The Second Conquest. The EU Free Trade Agreement with Colombia and Peru*. Amsterdam: Transnational Institute.

Garcia, M. 2015. The European Union and Latin America: 'Transformative Power Europe' Versus the Realities of Economic Interests. *Cambridge Review of International Relations* 28 (4): 621–640.

OIDHACO. 2010. *TLC entre UE y Colombia: una firma inoportuna, contraproducente e irresponsible*. International Office for Human Rights—Action on Colombia, 26 May.

Orbie, J., D. Martens, M. Oehri, and L. Van den Putte. 2017. Promoting Sustainable Development or Legitimising Free Trade? Civil Society Mechanisms in EU Trade Agreements. *Third World Thematics: A TWQ Journal*. https://doi.org/10.1080/23802014.2016.1294032

Schott, J. 2006. Free Trade Agreements and US Trade Policy: A Comparative Analysis of US Initiatives in Latin America, the Asia-Pacific Region, and the Middle East and North Africa. *International Trade Journal* 20 (2): 95–138.

Stevens, C., J. Kean, L. Bartels, and S. Woolcock. 2012. *European Union: Trade Agreement with Colombia and Peru*. Study Requested by the European Parliament, Policy Department DG External Policies, Brussels.

Woolcock, S., J. Keane, C. Stevens, and L. Bartels. 2012. *The Trade Chapter of the European Union Association Agreement with Central America*. Study Requested by the European Parliament, Policy Department DG External Policies, Brussels.

Wu, C.H. 2012. The Evolution of EU External Economic Law—Legal and Policy Changes. *EurAmerica* 42 (4): 753–839.

CHAPTER 4

Trade Agreements with ACP Countries

Abstract The EPAs are the most development-friendly PTAs concluded by the EU in the 2000s. The EU conceded the longest transition periods for market liberalization to ACP countries and concluded goods-only agreements with Sub-Saharan African states. Exporter and import-dependent interests did not have major stakes in the negotiations, due to the lack of domino effects with major trade powers and the low integration of these countries in GVCs. For these reasons, the politics of the EPA negotiations was mostly affected by European farmer organizations and NGOs. As an exception to these trends, import-dependent service industries actively participated in the Commission's consultations concerning the negotiations with CARIFORUM. Extensive mobilization of European NGOs, coupled with the lack of European offensive interests, resulted in substantial concessions from the EU to its ACP partners, and especially the African delegations. At the same time, CSOs obtained the inclusion of the most stringent norms concerning sustainable development and human rights in the agreements. On the producers' front, agricultural organizations were able to obtain protection for European-sensitive agricultural products, especially sugar. Service interest groups, in turn, pushed for liberalization commitments regarding key sectors relevant for European importers in the EPA negotiations with CARIFORUM.

Keywords Caribbean countries • Sub-Saharan Africa • European farmers • service industry • NGOs

A. Poletti, D. Sicurelli, *The Political Economy of Normative Trade Power Europe*, https://doi.org/10.1007/978-3-319-78864-7_4

4.1 Introduction

EPA negotiations with ACP countries started in the early 2000s as a response to the rulings of the WTO against the EU system that had been in place since 1975 of giving unilateral trade preferences to that group of former colonial countries. More specifically, the EU has carried out negotiations with sub-regional groupings of the ACP. Negotiations with the CARIFORUM[1] were concluded in December 2007, those with 17 West African states,[2] and with SADC[3] and EAC[4] in 2014.

As their name suggests, the EPAs have specific features as compared to the FTAs with Latin American and ASEAN countries. Thirty-nine out of the 49 least developed countries in the world are ACP countries, and most of them are in Sub-Saharan Africa. The decision of the negotiators to focus on the idea of partnership rather than on free trade was based on the fact that ACP countries are the least integrated in global markets and therefore need greater flexibility and support in terms of capacity building for lifting their trade barriers and adjusting to the EU's regulatory standards. The low level of integration of the ACP states in the global economy implies both a low level of participation in the GVCs and the relative isolation of the region from the network of major PTAs. For these reasons, the EPAs are the most asymmetric trade agreements negotiated by the EU. ACP countries mainly export raw materials, except for the CARIFORUM which mainly exports services. They are also less attractive for European and US investors and exporters than the Latin American and ASEAN states. Given these structural features of the ACP economy, the EPAs have mainly triggered the mobilization of NGOs concerned about the development implications of these agreements and farmer associations in the EU, which intensively lobbied the European Commission in order to obtain transition periods for the liberalization of EU markets in specific agricultural sectors. As an exception to the low mobilization of business groups, the services industry lobbied the European Commission in the negotiations with the CARIFORUM. Despite its lower interest in the Sub-Saharan markets, the services industry also actively participated in the Commission's consultations for the negotiations with the West African, SADC, and EAC states in order to push forward, indirectly, its global trade agenda.

Given the lack of offensive interests of the EU with respect to the ACP markets, the EU endorsed NGO demands to provide the partners with high flexibility and development support, consistent with the European Commission's 'differentiation' (Woolcock 2014, p. 36) approach to trade relations with developing countries. In turn, agricultural interests were able to obtain the inclusion of transition periods for the liberalization of sensitive sectors such as sugar and rice in the agreements. The services industry was influential in the shaping of a European position for the EU–CARIFORUM EPA.

This chapter is structured as follows. The first section introduces the legal framework of the EPAs, that is, the Cotonou Agreement between the EU and the ACP countries, and traces the WTO pressures for an end to the Lomé unilateral trade preferences scheme. The second part compares the major provisions included in the EPAs with Caribbean and African sub-regions of the ACP group. Finally, the third part analyses the political-economy dynamics behind the European negotiating position in the EPAs.

4.2 The Cotonou Agreement (2010) and the End of the Unilateral PTA

Following WTO rulings against the discriminatory effects of the European trade preferences towards ACP countries, the Cotonou Agreement (2010) sets the foundations for a new trade regime between the ACP group of states and the EU based on reciprocity, which would put an end to the preferential trade regime that had lasted since 1975.

In the negotiations for the Lomé I Convention (1975), the ACP countries obtained a preferential treatment based on non-reciprocity. In other words, the European Commission conceded preferential access to the European market to those countries without requiring them to lower their import duties. The convention gave a special status to a few sensitive goods for ACP countries, namely, bananas, beef, veal, and sugar. The banana protocol, more specifically, gave free access to specific quotas of bananas, while under the sugar products agreement the EU committed itself to buying a fixed quantity annually of sugar from ACP countries at high guaranteed prices in order to reduce the distorting effects of the EU subsidies under the Common Agricultural Policy. This long-lasting preferential treatment that contrasted with GATT rules has been explained in different ways. Flint (2009) regards it as a success of the ACP group in the shaping of the Lomé I Convention in 1975. To the surprise of the

EC negotiators, ACP states for the first time participated in the negotiations as a bloc, which increased the bargaining power of its members. Others, in contrast, have interpreted them as a form of control exerted by the European Commission over former colonies in the context of the Cold War. Steven (2008) notes that in fact the preferences did not provide factual advantages to the ACP countries. Sub-Saharan countries ironically gained more from exporting those products that were subject to restrictions under the preferential regime.

Three decades since its origins, this preferential trade regime was successfully challenged under the WTO dispute settlement mechanism. Colombia, Costa Rica, Guatemala, Nicaragua, and Venezuela, supported by the US, lodged a series of legal challenges in the WTO claiming that the EU preferences for bananas from ACP countries discriminated against Latin American banana producers and also hampered the expansion of US multinationals in this sector. In 1997 the WTO appellate body confirmed this allegation and ruled against the EU. Besides affecting the banana trade, the ruling had the effect of challenging the entire preference regime established at Lomé. The EU, in fact, instead of only revising its banana trade preferences, opted for a full revision of the Lomé regime. Indeed, because the banana regime was an artefact of overlapping and nested commitments, making the EU's banana regime fully WTO-compatible required changing the Lomé Convention, since a harmonized system of tariff-free bananas would have violated its promise of preferential access to the European market (Alter and Meunier 2006). As Daugbjerg and Swinbank (2008, p. 647) note, the knock-on effect of challenges to the banana regime was that the EU realized that its Lomé Convention was incompatible with its WTO commitments, leading to the decision to try and negotiate a series of WTO-compatible FTAs.

On this basis, the Cotonou Agreement (2000) aimed at setting the ground for trade agreements with the ACP countries based on reciprocal tariff removal. The Cotonou Agreement specifies that trade relations between the EU and the ACP countries must be both compatible with WTO law and oriented towards development cooperation. Article 34.4 of the agreement explains the relationship between the principles of reciprocal liberalization and differentiation according to the development needs of the partners, stating that 'Economic and trade cooperation shall be implemented in full conformity with the provisions of the WTO, including special and differential treatment, taking account of the Parties' mutual interests and their respective levels of development'.

In 2003 a new challenge against the EU was brought by Australia, Brazil, and Thailand. Those countries claimed that the EU sugar regime granted ACP sugar higher prices than sugar from other countries. Given the high industrial concentration of the sugar industry, the EU reacted to the dispute by refusing to make concessions during the consultations held with the complainants (Poletti and De Bièvre 2014). The panel and then the Appellate Body of the WTO in 2004 and 2014 reiterated that the EU had to reform its sugar policy. As a response, the EU had to put an end to the Sugar Protocol and, in 2006, adopt the sugar sector reform, which implied that the EU cut preferential prices for ACP sugar by 39% by 2010. In turn, the EPA negotiations offered the EU a new opportunity to obtain special treatment for the European sugar producers.

The WTO conceded a waiver until the end of 2007 in order to support the transition from the preferential scheme and negotiate new reciprocal liberalization schemes. While negotiations with the CARIFORUM went smoothly and led to an EPA in 2008, negotiations with African members stalled until the end of the waiver. A major obstacle for starting the negotiations was the difficulty of the African members in agreeing on the configuration of the regional groupings that should negotiate with the EU. Given the presence of multiple overlapping sub-regional organizations in Africa, most of the sub-Saharan African states are at the same time members of multiple groupings. Therefore, they appeared reluctant to select which region should represent them in the negotiations.[5] Thus, in order to comply with the WTO ruling within the deadline imposed by the WTO, by the end of 2007 and in 2008 the EU was forced to conclude the first interim deals with single Sub-Saharan African states and with regions that differed from those that were originally selected for negotiating with the EU. Finally, in 2014 the EU formalized the EPAs with SADC, West Africa and the EAC. The European Commission has since then explained the differences between the single EPAs by referring to its differentiation policy. The fragmentation of the ACP in sub-regions weakened the leverage of the group in the negotiations. Since each of the regions negotiated separately with the EU, 'it is conventional to refer to the EU in the singular and the ACP in the plural, since this reflects the negotiation reality' (Stevens 2008).

4.3 The EPAs with the CARIFORUM and Sub-Saharan Countries

The main difference between the EPA with the CARIFORUM and those concluded with West, East, and South African states is that the former is a comprehensive agreement, which covers goods and services liberalization, investment, IPR, and other trade-related matters that the Lomé Conventions had never addressed. The others are goods-only deals, mainly covering liberalization of trade in goods, but also including labour and environmental protection standards and human right clauses, as required by the Cotonou Agreement, and leaving 'behind the border issues' for further negotiations (see Table 4.1).

As far as trade in goods is concerned, all the EPAs are meant to fulfil the GATT requirement of reciprocal liberalization of 'substantially all the trade' between the parties. Article XXIC, paragraph 8 of the GATT, requires members that are negotiating PTAs to lift duties and trade barriers on 'substantially all the trade' between the parties. Paragraph 5 states that trade barriers should be lifted within a 'reasonable length of time'. Given the vague wording of these conditions and the fact that WTO jurisprudence does not clearly establish the exact percentage of trade that corresponds to this concept, European negotiators proposed to the ACP countries that approximately 90% of the trade lines and trade volume between the EU and those countries should be liberalized. As a development cooperation measure, the European Commission initially proposed a commitment of the EU to liberalize approximately 100% of European goods and a requirement for Sub-Saharan African states to liberalize about 80% of their goods (Sicurelli 2010). The number of sensitive products protected by the EU and the ACP partners, though, varies according to the single EPAs.

The EU provides duty-free, quota-free access of 100% of its tariff lines to EAC and to all the members of SADC with the exception of South Africa. The agreement offers duty-free quota-free access to the EU of 95% of South African goods. The agreement with the CARIFORUM includes rice and sugar among the sensitive products of the EU, while the agreement with West Africa protects EU dairy products, rice, sugar, and meat. As far as market access to the partners of the EU is concerned, West Africa and EAC members can protect more goods than the other partners. The two regions have the highest number of low-income countries as compared to the other ACP regions. West Africa, above all, has ten low-income member states and six lower-middle-income countries, while EAC has four low-income countries and one lower-middle-income country. Members of both West Africa and EAC are required to liberalize 75% of tariff lines, which amounts to about 80% of trade volume. West Africa has a 20-year timeframe after the agreement enters into force for liberalizing most of its tariff lines, while EAC has 15 years and 25 for sensitive products. The CARIFORUM commits to liberalization of 90.2% of tariff lines in 5–15 years, with most of the liberalization in the first 10 years. CARIFORUM states received a 25-year transition time for the liberalization of sensitive products. Finally, SADC (the wealthier region in Sub-Saharan Africa, with one low-income country, two lower-middle-income countries, and three upper-middle-income countries) has to liberalize 97.7% of tariff lines in nine years, which corresponds to 85.6% of trade volume.

The EU–CARIFORUM EPA differs from the other EPAs in its inclusion of a MFN clause, which is applicable to future trade partners of the EU and the CARIFORUM. On the one hand, the EU 'shall accord to commercial presences and investors of the Signatory CARIFORUM States a treatment no less favourable than the most favourable treatment applicable to like commercial presences and investors ***of any third country*** with whom it concludes an economic integration agreement after the signature of this Agreement' (emphasis added). On the other hand, the Caribbean members 'shall accord to the commercial presences and investors of the EC Party a treatment no less favourable than the most favourable treatment applicable to like commercial presences and investors of ***any major trading economy*** with whom they conclude an economic integration agreement' (Article 70). The wording of this clause provides a certain degree of asymmetry in favour of the Caribbean states, since the CARIFORUM states obtain first-class access to the most favourable treatment the EU may give in the future to any third country, while the clause only applies to future agreements between the CARIFORUM and any major trading economy, while it excludes future trade agreements with lower-income countries.

The provisions included in the EPAs on trade defence also differ from the provisions included in the other trade agreements analysed in this volume for the presence of an infant industry protection clause. The protection of infant industries in developing countries is compatible with WTO law and is recognized as a form of special and differential treatment for developing countries. The EPAs with the CARIFORUM and EAC provide protection to infant industries for ten years, while EPAs with West Africa and SADC do so for eight years.

Each of the EPAs also includes flexible rules of origin, based on diagonal cumulation. This type of cumulation operates between more than two countries that have concluded FTAs with identical rules of origins and provisions for cumulation between them. Regional cumulation is a form of diagonal cumulation and applies to members of a regional group of countries. The cumulation provision included in the EU–CARIFORUM EPA is especially favourable for the Caribbean members since it may be extended to neighbouring developing countries, including Mexico. Each of the EPAs, though, includes exceptions to the rule, aimed at protecting sensitive EU products. The EU–CARIFORUM EPA includes a time-limited exclusion from diagonal cumulation for rice, sugar, and products with high sugar content. The EPA with SADC also includes a time-limited exclusion from diagonal cumulation for some agricultural products from South Africa. The EPAs with West Africa and EAC also exclude agricultural products from diagonal cumulation.

As mentioned above, the major difference between the EPA with the Caribbean countries and the agreements concluded by Sub-Saharan African countries is that only the first one includes chapters on services, investment, government procurement, and IPR. The other EPAs include *rendez-vous* clauses on these matters. As far as service liberalization is concerned, CARIFORUM states agree to liberalize from 60% to 75% of their services, including key sectors such as telecommunications, transport, tourism, manufacturing, and environmental services. Thus the Caribbean states accept a WTO-plus degree of service liberalization. The EU, in turn, commits to liberalize 90% of services (Kategekwa 2013). The provisions on investment liberalization included in the EU–CARIFORUM EPA are asymmetric, since they allow the Caribbean members to protect sensitive sectors. The EPA has no provisions concerning an investor-state dispute settlement (ISDS) mechanism. Moreover, the agreement includes soft provisions on competitiveness in government procurement, that is to say transparency measures. The EPA does not include liberalization commitments between the parties. The EPA with the Caribbean states includes high standards of IPR. It extends the existing protection for wines and spirits under the TRIPS Agreement to all other goods potentially protectable by geographical indications. The agreement, though, has adopted a soft language on technology transfer, protection of biological resources, and traditional knowledge, which are the sectors that are most relevant for

Caribbean countries (Robinson and Gibson 2011). The EPA with SADC, furthermore, has a protocol on geographical indications that specifies the products protected by the EU and South Africa. On the EU side, 251 products, including 105 agricultural products and foodstuff, 5 beers, 120 wines, and 21 spirits are protected. South Africa, in contrast, protects 105 products and 102 wines.

All the EPAs contain provisions on cooperation on labour and environmental protection. Each of them (except for the SADC EPA) has a monitoring mechanism that involves joint committees or consultative committees. In contrast to the trade agreements with Vietnam and Singapore (see Chap. 5), though, they do not include provisions on the timing and frequency of the meetings. Even though it does not have a separate chapter on sustainable development, the EPA with the CARIFORUM stands for its far-reaching provisions concerning labour and environmental protection. It is the only PTA that applies dispute settlement provisions to sustainable development. However, it does not allow the suspension of trade concessions or financial cooperation in the event that one of the parties violates sustainable development standards.

Finally, in respect to human rights, all the EPAs have non-execution clauses, which allow the parties to take any appropriate measures in case of violation of human rights; these are considered essential elements of the agreements.

4.4 Tracing the Process of EU Preference Shaping in the Negotiations with ACP Countries

The negotiating positions of the European Commission concerning the EPAs mainly accommodated pressures from NGOs and agricultural organizations. Import-dependent interests were almost absent in the consultations, as illustrated by the fact that a European Commission official involved in the EPA negotiations claimed to be unfamiliar with Eurocommerce. Organizations representing the interests of European services providers are an exception to this broader trend.[6]

A broad and internally differentiated network of NGOs actively lobbied the European Commission from the early stages of the negotiations. The network involved the most radical opponents of the EPAs, grouped into the No EPA campaign, as well as NGOs that aimed at influencing the negotiating positions of the European Commission in a more constructive

Table 4.1 The EPAs between the EU and ACP countries

	EU–CARIFORUM (2007)	*EU–SADC (2014)*	*EU–West Africa (2014)*	*EU–EAC (2014)*
Market access to the EU	Tariff elimination, except for rice and sugar.	Tariff elimination (excluding sensitive agricultural products for South Africa).	Tariff elimination.	Tariff elimination.
Market access to the partner	Liberalization of 90.2% of tariff lines in 5–15 years (25 for sensitive products). MFN clause: 'CARIFORUM states shall accord to EU trade and investment partners a treatment no less favourable than that applicable to partners from other major economies.'	Liberalization of 97.7% of tariff lines in 10 years (excluding agriculture and fishery products).	Liberalization of 75% of tariff lines in 20 years (excluding sensitive products).	Liberalization of 74.4% of tariff lines in 15 years (25 for sensitive products).
Anti-dumping	Infant industry protection clause for 10 years.	Infant industry protection clause for 8 years.	Infant industry protection clause for 8 years.	Infant industry protection clause for 10 years.
Rules of origin	Diagonal cumulation. Cumulation may be extended to neighbouring developing countries, including Mexico, upon CARIFORUM request. Time-limited exclusion from diagonal cumulation for rice, sugar, and products with high sugar content.	Diagonal cumulation. Time-limited exclusion from diagonal cumulation for some agricultural products from South Africa.	Diagonal cumulation. Agricultural products are excluded.	Diagonal cumulation. Agricultural products are excluded.
Trade in services	CARIFORUM states agree to liberalize from 60% to 75% of services, including telecommunications, transport, tourism, manufacturing, and environmental services, while the EU concedes to liberalize 90% of services.	Rendez-vous clause.	Rendez-vous clause.	Rendez-vous clause.

(*continued*)

Table 4.1 (continued)

	EU–CARIFORUM (2007)	*EU–SADC (2014)*	*EU–West Africa (2014)*	*EU–EAC (2014)*
Investment	Investment liberalizations (CARIFORUM excludes sensitive sectors). No ISDS.	Rendez-vous clause.	Rendez-vous clause.	Rendez-vous clause.
Government procurement	Transparency measures, but no liberalization commitments.	Rendez-vous clause.	Rendez-vous clause.	Rendez-vous clause.
State-owned enterprises (SOEs)	Not treated.	Not treated.	Not treated.	Not treated.
IPR	Treated in the context of cooperation on innovation, with transition periods between 2014 and 2021. Rendez-vous clause on the specification of geographical indications.	Protocol on geographical indications.	Rendez-vous clause.	Rendez-vous clause.
Sustainable development	Cotonou Agreement calls for ratification and enforcement of all the core UN environmental and labour conventions. Joint committees or consultative committees. Enforcement provision: dispute settlement mechanism.	Cotonou Agreement calls for ratification and enforcement of all the core UN environmental and labour conventions.	Cotonou Agreement calls for ratification and enforcement of all the core UN environmental and labour conventions. Joint committees or consultative committees.	Cotonou Agreement calls for ratification and enforcement of all the core UN environmental and labour conventions. Joint committees or consultative committees.
Human rights	Linkage with the Cotonou Agreement: mandatory political dialogue in non-urgent cases; suspension of the agreement as a last-resort measure.	Linkage with the Cotonou Agreement: mandatory political dialogue in non-urgent cases; suspension of the agreement as a last-resort measure.	Linkage with the Cotonou Agreement: mandatory political dialogue in non-urgent cases; suspension of the agreement as a last-resort measure.	Linkage with the Cotonou Agreement: mandatory political dialogue in non-urgent cases; suspension of the agreement as a last-resort measure.

way. European development NGOs joined their pressures with African NGOs. Since late 2002 a group of European and international NGOs started to express their critical positions against the decision of the EU to negotiate the EPAs (Dür and De Bièvre 2007). Development NGOs shared the concern over the implications for development of the end of the Lomé preferential system for ACP countries. Above all, they criticized the attempt of the EU to push forward in the EPA negotiations a much broader agenda than that imposed by the WTO rulings. According to these organizations, the EU was pursuing in the context of the EPAs the trade interests it had failed to promote in the Doha Round, concerning not only market access but also trade in services, investments, the Singapore issues (competition, government procurement, trade facilitation, and investment), and sustainable development. The Singapore issues, originally included in the agenda of the Doha negotiations, were excluded from the talks in the Cancun meeting in 2003, when developing countries expressed their opposition to an agreement on those issues (Poletti 2012). Following their exclusion from the multilateral negotiations, the EU had tried to promote agreements with ACP countries on those topics. NGOs also contested the lack of coherence between the European stance on reciprocal liberalization and its practice of subsidizing farmers in the context of the Common Agricultural Policy. Furthermore, a coalition of European development and environmental NGOs and trade unions promoted the inclusion of high sustainability standards in the EPAs.

The EPA negotiations also triggered the mobilization of import-competing interests, mainly organizations representing European agricultural interests. The EU and ACP economies are less complementary than those of the EU and ASEAN members, due to the fact that agricultural goods are sensitive for both parties. Protectionist groups in the agricultural sector mobilized in order to achieve trade agreements that would contrast the negative effects of the CAP reform required by developing countries in the Doha round. Finally, since the Caribbean states are the only net exporters of services in the ACP group, service interest groups actively lobbied the European Commission in order to contribute to shaping its negotiating position in the CARIFORUM. They also participated in the consultation exercises of the European Commission for the negotiations with African delegations, but did not obtain the inclusion of services in the agenda.

As Heron and Murray-Evans (2017) notice, despite its initial preference for comprehensive agreements, the EU had to accept to conclude trade-only deals with Sub-Saharan African countries. According to the authors, in this case 'the EU has been unable to translate its preponderance of market power and considerable diplomatic resources into a more favourable outcome of the negotiations' (p. 358). The political-economy dynamics behind the EPA negotiations contribute to address this puzzle and demonstrate that, in contrast to the other regional groupings, the Sub-Saharan African region is mostly indirectly relevant for the EU's global trade agenda (see Table 4.2). Business interest groups, especially in the sector of services, did promote a deep liberalization agenda on a broad number of issues including services and the Singapore issues in the negotiations with Sub-Saharan African countries, and had to withdraw its requests following the African delegations' opposition. The lack of interest in exporting to the Sub-Saharan region, though, made this negotiating 'failure' (Heron and Murray-Evans 2017, p. 341) relatively acceptable to those groups and, ultimately, to the EU negotiators.

4.4.1 *The Politics of EU Negotiations with the CARIFORUM*

The EPA with the CARIFORUM was negotiated between 2004 and 2007. The CARIFORUM group differs from the other sub-regions of the ACP because most of its members classify as high- and middle-income countries, and only one member, Haiti, is a least developed country. For this reason, with the exception of Haiti, CARIFORUM members were not eligible for the Everything but Arms initiative implemented by the EU since 2001, which provides preferential market access to least developed countries. Thus they were more interested than states in other ACP regions in negotiating a PTA with the EU. In turn, CARIFORUM enjoys greater supranational authority and bureaucratic capacity to negotiate than the other members of the ACP group (Heron 2011). Its members are highly open to trade and more familiar than other ACP states with negotiations on matters such as WTO compatibility, trade in services, and other trade-related issues. Furthermore, the dominance of the neoliberal belief in the CARIFORUM negotiators facilitated an early conclusion of the EU–CARIFORUM deal (Nyaga Munyi 2016). When the EPA negotiations started, they had already negotiated on those issues within the Caribbean Community (CARICOM) and were also tackling those issues in the negotiations for the Free Trade Area of the Americas (Vahl 2011). Yet, the relationship between the EU and CARIFORUM is asymmetric. On the one hand, the EU is a highly attractive market. It was so especially during the EU–CARIFORUM negotiations, which ended before the explosion of the global financial crisis that hit European economies. On the other hand, in the words of a Caribbean negotiator of the EPA, CARIFORUM negotiations are 'vulnerable to external shocks; having high external debts; economies that are significantly skewed towards services; and relying on the United States as their major trading partner' (Spence 2009).

In 2004, 19% of goods imported to CARIFORUM came from the EU, while 18% of the goods exported from the region were directed to the EU (Borrmann and Busse 2007). The Caribbean states had benefited enormously from the unilateral preferences conceded by the EU, since 95% of the goods exported by CARIFORUM to the EU were subject to those preferences (Heron 2011). Above all, Caribbean countries were highly dependent on agricultural exports to the EU, which represents the second largest destination of those products after the US (European Community–Caribbean Region 2008). The US imported approximately 55% of the region's total exports (Heron 2011). Caribbean states mainly export raw materials to the EU, such as fuel and mining products, agricultural products mainly concentrated on a few tropical commodities such as bananas and sugar, rum, and minerals. The major partner of the EU in the CARIFORUM is the Dominican Republic, followed by the Bahamas, Jamaica, and Trinidad and Tobago.

In the early 2000s, EU-exported goods to the region mainly included boats, ships, cars, phone equipment, milk and cream, and spirit drinks. However, more than half of the export flow from CARIFORUM to the EU was derived from services, especially tourism, which was not covered by the Cotonou Agreement (Heron 2011).

During the negotiations for the EU–CARIFORUM development EPA, NGOs mobilized in order to affect the Commission's position. The 'Stop EPA' movement was born in 2004, when the negotiations with the Caribbean states started. It was formally launched in both Lusaka and London. It involved the foundations of the Accra-based Africa Trade Network and a number of European NGOs that criticized the small development component of the negotiations. However, those pressures to stop the EPA negotiations proved unsuccessful since they lacked the support of a large-scale grass-roots campaign (Girvan 2010).

In order to respond to those protests, both the EU and the CARIFORUM organized mechanisms to engage non-state actors in preparation for the EPA negotiations (Montoute 2016). On the Caribbean side, a Non-State Actor Advisory Panel was created in 2005 in order to facilitate participation of Caribbean organizations such as community-based organizations, trade unions, women's groups, farmer associations, and business organizations. On the EU side, the Commission only started organizing consultation tables with CSOs at the end of the negotiations with CARIFORUM, in 2007, when the EPAs had become a highly political issue in Europe (Sicurelli 2010). The impact of pressures of European interest groups and NGOs can be traced by analysing the process that led to the negotiating position of the European Commission on particular chapters within the EU–CARIFORUM EPA.

4.4.1.1 Market Access, Rules of Origin, and Anti-dumping

Due to the absence of offensive interests of the EU in its relations with the CARIFORUM (Faber and Orbie 2007), negotiations on trade in goods mainly mobilized protectionist interests in the agricultural sector and NGOs. European exporter organizations only mobilized in order to obtain access to the Dominican Republic equal to what the US had gained in the agreement it had already signed with the country.

Farmers' organizations, especially from France, Spain, Poland, Portugal, and Italy, lobbied their governments and the European Commission in order to obtain exemptions from tight liberalization schedules of European sugar, bananas, and rice.[7] French farmers especially lobbied for protection of banana production in the French overseas department (Martinique and Guadeloupe) (Sicurelli 2010). In order to address these demands, the Commission obtained from CARIFORUM the designation of sugar and rice as EU's sensitive products.[8] The negotiating position of the EU, on the contrary, excluded bananas among the sensitive products.[9] In this respect, though, the farmer organizations, with the support of European environmental NGOs, were able to obtain stringent sanitary standards on pesticide levels in the sector of bananas (LaForce 2014).

As far as market access to CARIFORUM was concerned, the European Parliament and key member states such as the UK supported NGOs' demands for the inclusion of long transition periods for tariff elimination for Caribbean sensitive products. The EU conceded the protection of sensitive products from CARIFORUM over the longest transition period ever included in PTAs. Only EAC would subsequently obtain analogous conditions for sensitive products from the EU.

European exporters' interests were mainly confined to the Dominican Republic, which had already concluded a trade agreement with the US and CA (CAFTA-DR) in 2005. Voicing their demands, the European Commission's DG Trade asked for better market access conditions than the US and CA countries had in the Dominican Republic, and obtained more extensive liberalization from the country than from the other CARIFORUM members, on a par with the liberalization included in the CAFTA-DR (Gammage 2017). These demands confirmed CARIFORUM concerns for the implications of the precedent-setting FTA with the US for the EPA negotiations (Byron and Levis 2007). Furthermore, European exporter and investor organizations were able to obtain the most favourable treatment applicable to other major trading economies that would in the future conclude trade agreements with the CARIFORUM states. This clause, according to an official of DG Trade, represents an 'insurance against potential trade discrimination' of European exporters '*vis a vis* significant third countries, in circumstances where the EU had been the major supplier of development assistance of 40 years' (European Commission 2008a). This formulation of MFN drew contestation among other trade partners, especially Brazil, for its potential implications for the competitiveness of emerging countries in the region (Sauvé and Ward 2009). The EU also endorsed the request from development NGOs (Oxfam 2005) to include a flexibility measure such as an infant industry clause in the anti-dumping chapter. Negotiations on rules of origin also mobilized an alliance of NGOs (Stop Epa 2007) that voiced the request of CARIFORUM delegations of regional cumulation, which would facilitate transborder regional production among Caribbean and Latin American countries. The association representing importer associations, Eurocommerce (2007), consistent with the position it had adopted with respect to the Doha Round, also supported flexible rules of origin in its negotiations with all the ACP countries. Despite COPA-COGECA's demands for 'controls on imports', including 'effective rules of origins' (Agritrade 2007), the Commission endorsed the CARIFORUM request for flexible rules of origin based on broad cumulation possibilities.

4.4.1.2 Trade in Services, Investments, and Public Procurement

The preference of the European Commission for the inclusion of an ambitious chapter on liberalization of trade in services, investments, and public procurement mirrored the new global trade agenda of the EU following the communication by the European Commission (2006) titled 'Global Europe: Competing in the World'. This communication had inaugurated an aggressive approach of the EU towards penetrating international markets though the liberalization of services and investments. The preference of the EU for the negotiation of a comprehensive trade agreement with CARIFORUM, in turn, was the response to the acceleration of the US's competitive liberalization policy and to the failure of the pressures of the EU to include the Singapore issues in the Doha Development Agenda in 2003.

According to Heron (2011), the EU had little to gain from the EPA with the CARIFORUM in strict commercial terms. Yet, the EPA with the Caribbean did have the potential to affect the EU service sector, since CARIFORUM members were the only net suppliers of services among ACP countries (Laforce 2014). Following pressures from the European Services Forum (2007a), which engaged in intense lobbying activities throughout the negotiations promoting extensive commitments on services liberalization and investment, DG Trade demanded of its Caribbean counterparts conditions on service liberalization that would put the EU at least in a position of parity with its most significant competitors in the region (Heron and Siles-Brügge 2012). The CARIFORUM delegation concurred with the EU that, as service economies, its members would take little advantage from an agreement addressing only trade in goods (Spence 2009) and agreed to liberalize up to 75% of services, including key sectors such as telecommunications, transport, tourism, manufacturing, and environmental services, while the EU conceded to liberalize 90% of its member countries' services. The wording of the MFN clause, which requires the Caribbean states to accord to the commercial presences and investors of the EC Party a treatment no less favourable than the most favourable treatment applicable to any major trading economy with whom they conclude an economic integration agreement, also addresses the interests of the European service sector.

The decision of the EU to include services and Singapore issues in the agenda of the EPA negotiations with the CARIFORUM raised harsh reactions among NGOs (Deckwirth 2005; Dür and De Bièvre 2007). They pointed to a contradiction in the discourse of the European Commission that repeatedly claimed to be bound by the WTO to reform its relations with the ACP states but, in fact, insisted on the inclusion of WTO-plus rules. From the perspective of Stop Epa (2007), 'the EC has adamantly insisted on including in EPAs the kinds of rules on investment, competition, and government procurement that they previously failed to get inserted into the WTO'. Also, environmental NGOs expressed their opposition to the inclusion of investment liberalization and government procurement discipline in the EPA. According to FOE (2006), '[t]he EU failed to push investment through at the WTO and is now trying to force it through the backdoor with EPA'.

4.4.1.3 IPR, Sustainable Development, and Human Rights

Backing NGOs' criticism of the WTO-plus scope of the EPA, the Center for International Environmental Law (2008) claimed that even 'the inclusion of intellectual property in the EPAs was not necessary to comply with the WTO rules on preferential treatment for goods from ACP countries'. According to Oxfam (2008), '[t]he intellectual property provisions in the Caribbean "full EPA" support positions that Europe has advocated (and developing countries, including the Africa Group, have strongly resisted) in the World Intellectual Property Organization'.

The EU had an extensive system of protection of geographical indications in comparison to CARIFORUM countries, which had never established a full system of identifying and accrediting geographical indications. On these bases, development NGOs criticizing the attempt of the EU to secure the economic profit of major European multinationals by enforcing IPR failed in influencing the negotiating position of the EU. Nevertheless, the CARIFORUM negotiators acknowledged that an agreement on innovation and IPR would help its members to develop competitive advantages by differentiating its production. In turn, though, they asked the EU to 'ensure that the EPA does not impair a state's capacity to promote access to medicines, protect public health and nutrition' (Spence 2009). The EU addressed this demand by including a reference to facilitation of technology transfer between CARIFORUM and the EU (Art. 142). Nevertheless, the stark contrast between the generic language used for the agreement on protection of biological resources and traditional knowledge and the high standards of protection on copyrights, geographical indications, and strict enforcement provisions concerning IPR in the agreement confirms that the European negotiators tried to pursue the broader agenda on IPR in the negotiations with the Caribbean that they had promoted in the context of the World Intellectual Property Organization.

The Cotonou Agreement, which treats sustainable development as the overarching objective of the partnership with the ACP, gave the European negotiators a legal framework to promote tight sustainability norms. The failure of the attempt of the EU to push forward labour and environmental rights as a negotiating issue in the Doha round also motivated the European negotiators to promote high standards in this sector within inter-regional trade deals. A coalition of trade unions,[10] environmental (FOE 2006) and development NGOs (Oxfam 2006) interested in upholding European sustainability standards especially lobbied for the inclusion of labour and environmental protection norms in the EPA with the CARIFORUM. On this basis, and given the interest of the CARIFORUM members in concluding an ambitious comprehensive agreement,[11] the EU was able to obtain the most binding norms on sustainable development ever included in the EU FTAs. The inclusion of the dispute settlement mechanism in case of violation of labour and environmental norms was also possible due to the fact that the Dominican Republic had already agreed upon a similar mechanism in the context of the CAFTA-DR in 2005 (Kerremans and Gistelinck 2009), thereby setting a precedent for future agreements involving the Caribbean states. The Caribbean trade unions, NGOs, and small- to micro-sized industries supported high sustainability standards but complained about the lack of aid disbursement from the EU in support of those provisions (Byron and Lewis 2007).

Finally, with respect to human rights, the Cotonou Agreement includes the most elaborate consultation procedure required by EU inter-regional cooperation agreements, which requires a mandatory political dialogue in non-urgent cases as a preliminary step, and the suspension of the agreement as a last-resort measure. These provisions compelled the EU to include highly binding provisions concerning human rights in the EPA, as compared to the other FTAs negotiated by the EU.

4.4.2 *The Politics of EU Negotiations with Sub-Saharan African States*

As in the case of the CARIFORUM, the integration of Sub-Saharan African states negotiating the EPA with the EU in the GVCs is extremely low (Nord 2015). Furthermore, the main international trade partners of this region include emerging countries such as China and India, while the US and other major trade actors have marginal trade interests in the area. As Woolcock (2014) puts it, the US is not competing with the EU to conclude a PTA with those countries. Above all, Sub-Saharan Africa is not an attractive region for European exports. Trade flows between Europe and Sub-Saharan African countries have decreased since the 1970s. This trend was evident even under the unilateral preferential scheme established by the Lomè Conventions. The growing role of China and India as partners of those countries since the 2000s has further diminished the significance of the EU as a trade player in the region. In 2017 Günter Nooke, Angela Merkel's representative to Africa, went so far as to comment that the current state of trade between Africa and the EU is 'almost irrelevant', beyond natural resources such as cocoa and coffee beans, 'and some diamond-cutting in Botswana' (Tempest 2017).

As in the case of the CARIFORUM EPA, due to the marginal interest of exporters (with a few sector-specific exceptions) and import-dependent groups in the region, the EPAs with West, East, and South Africa mainly mobilized NGOs and farmer organizations. In contrast to the negotiations with the Caribbean countries, furthermore, service organizations did not have a relevant stake in the trade talks with Sub-Saharan African countries.

4.4.2.1 Market Access, Rules of Origin, and Anti-dumping

Following the conclusion of the EU–CARIFORUM EPA, the European Commission organized three major consultation meetings with civil society, in 2008 (European Commission 2008b), 2011 (European Commission 2011b), and 2012 (European Commission 2012b). Organizations that participated in the consultations included a large number of development NGOs, foundations, and associations of sector-specific industries. As far as the business sector was concerned, it was mainly protectionist groups that actively participated in each of the consultations, especially the International Confederation of European Beet Growers, the Comité Européen des Fabricants de Sucre, and the Comité Européen de Liaison des Commerces Agricoles et Agro-alimentaires. The financial crisis that had hit Europe in 2008 also contributed to strengthening the protectionist interests in the negotiations with the African states.

The only exporter association that appeared especially interested in the negotiation was the European Dairy Association, which represents the interests of exporters of milk powder. Finally, the European Services Association actively participated in the consultations, together with a group of sector-specific organizations interested in the import and distribution of African goods, such as the European Association of Sugar Traders, the European Cocoa Association, the European Fruit and Vegetables Trade, and the Comité Européen Interprofessionnel du Thon Tropical.

Protectionist interests in Europe mainly found support in the Eastern and Southern member states, which had no historical obligation towards ACP countries. Agricultural organizations were also very influential in France, even though the country is home to CSOs that strongly mobilized against the EPAs (Sicurelli 2010). The major success achieved by the agricultural organizations was that the EPAs did not put an end to the trade-distorting subsidies allocated by the EU to farmers. Moreover, protectionist interest groups were able to obtain transition periods for the liberalization of EU sugar and exceptions to flexible rules of origins in the agricultural sector, especially with respect to imported goods from West Africa, EAC, and South Africa. In this sector, pressures from import-competing groups prevailed over demands from NGOs concerned about the development implications of the EPAs (Stop Epa 2007; Oxfam 2008) and of European academics who argued in favour of flexible rules of origins also in those sectors (Euractiv 2008). In addition, a joint report written by the Commission of the African Union and the UN Economic Commission for Africa (2007) had called for simple rules of origin, with no exceptions. According to the report, '[t]here should be a move away from product-specific rules of origin which are difficult to administer to more general rules of application, value addition or level of materials used'. Despite these demands, the EU promoted exceptions to agricultural products for the cumulation of rules of origin.

A coalition of West African CSOs mobilized in order to 'to ensure that whatever the outcome of an EPA was gonna be, it was not gonna be an FTA' (Trommer 2014, p. 11). More specifically, they refused the EU argument that, in order to fulfil the GATT 'substantially all the trade' condition, African countries should liberalize approximately 80% of their trade volume. Their proposal, in turn, was that Western African countries could liberalize at most 70% of their market (*ibidem*). The EU, though, refused to change its interpretation and obtained from its West African counterparts a commitment to liberalize about 80% of their trade volume.

Where access to the West African market was concerned, a tangible impact of the intense lobbying efforts of the European Dairy Association is that the EPA with West Africa imposes a 5% cap on duties for milk powder in West African countries. This cap de facto prevents West Africa from prioritizing local production (Europeanmilkboard 2016). The Economic Justice Network ultimately felt that the EU had imposed its conditions on the West African delegations, which 'suddenly reversed' their 'position and made serious and incomprehensible concessions to the EU' (Weinhardt 2014).

Pressures from European NGOs (Oxfam 2008) and African states for flexible anti-dumping rules, instead, contributed to the inclusion of infant industry protection clauses for variable transition periods of eight to ten years according to the trade partner. South Africa especially promoted the right of a country among those participating in the negotiations to protect its infant industries (Brundsen 2008).

Finally, the European Services Forum tried, without success, to promote the inclusion of service liberalization requirements in the EPAs with Sub-Saharan African countries. Despite its relatively low interest in the African services sector, the European Services Forum considered the EPAs as an arena to push forward a wider global agenda.[12] In contrast to the CARIFORUM members, delegations from Sub-Saharan Africa were not willing to negotiate comprehensive agreements including WTO-plus commitments.[13] The development NGOs and environmental associations (Euractiv 2008), supported by the 'usual suspects' (the UK, the Netherlands, Sweden, and Denmark), also argued against the proposal to include services, investment, and government procurement provisions in the agreements, based on the argument that Sub-Saharan African countries need more time, financial support, and capacity building to adjust to EU regulatory standards in these issues (Sicurelli 2010). The British government under the Blair leadership, despite its firm preference for liberalization, was vulnerable to NGO pressures, especially from Oxfam.[14]

4.4.2.2 IPR, Sustainable Development, and Human Rights

European stakeholders were divided on the inclusion of IPR in the EPAs. Development NGOs and think tanks lobbied for the conclusion of goods-only agreements with African countries that would not include a chapter on IPR. On the contrary, European farmer organizations aimed at strengthening protection of EU's geographical indications and IPR as an import control measure. In general, though, most respondents to the European Commission's public consultation on the Future of European Trade Policy in 2010, including NGOs and various sector industry associations, commented that, for the ACP group, 'a standard approach to negotiations cannot be adopted given differences in the level of development' (European Commission 2010).

African delegations expressed their firm opposition to the inclusion of IPR provisions in the agreement (Suvye Phiri 2009). Even South Africa, which had the most extensive national system of protection of IPR on the continent, did not consider itself sufficiently prepared to negotiate those provisions (Center for International Environmental Law 2008). The EU did not endorse the request from SADC countries to include positive commitments regarding the protection of traditional knowledge and folklore in the agreement (Suvye Phiri 2009), while it obtained from South Africa an agreement on geographical indications for a list of goods including agricultural, foodstuff, and spirits.

With respect to sustainable development, African delegations refused to negotiate binding provisions comparable to those included in the EU–CARIFORUM EPA. For this reason, negotiators on both sides 'focused first and foremost on reaching an acceptable deal for all, concentrating on key substantive provisions of the agreements by the EU's imposed October 2014 deadline' (Bilal and Ramdoo 2016). Discussions on labour rights and environmental protection, therefore, were left to the last stage of the negotiations. Another obstacle to the negotiation of binding sustainable development norms was represented by the growing role of China as an attractive partner for trade and investment in African states. In 2014, when the EPA negotiations with African delegations were concluded, the role of China in Africa was dramatically changed in comparison to the early stages of the negotiations. The Chinese had signed numerous bilateral trade agreements with African countries, including South Africa. Since those agreements excluded any reference to sustainable development, the African negotiators may have considered the inclusion of those provisions in a trade agreement unnecessary. Two leaders of West African states, namely, Abdoulaye Wade, the president of Senegal, and Shamsuddeen Usman, Nigeria's minister of finance, clarified the positions of African governors on this issue. More specifically, according to the president of Senegal, 'It's clear that Africa rejects the EPA', while Africa is more open to the 'more pragmatic' attitude of Chinese companies (Castle 2007). Nigeria's minister of finance further commented that 'Nigeria is becoming a beautiful bride. What is happening is the Chinese, the Koreans, everyone is coming around, and if European companies do not wake up, they will see that most of the best businesses are taken' (The Economist 2007). A further reason why the binding enforcement rules included in the EU–CARIFORUM EPA with respect to sustainable development were not included in the EPAs with African countries is that the Korea–EU agreement, concluded in 2009 and meant to represent a benchmark for all the future PTAs negotiated by the EU, has a softer chapter on sustainable development in contrast to the EU–CARIFORUM EPA. This outcome raised concerns of European NGOs (FOE 2006) and trade unions,[15] as well as Friends of the Earth (FOE 2006), which aimed at a more ambitious commitment of the parties on sustainable development. Pressures from European development and environmental NGOs for binding sustainability norms had only a marginal impact. According to Langan (2014), the EU adopted a co-optative strategy with respect to NGOs. It tied the discourse on decent work with free market policies in order to represent its calls for liberalization as being morally legitimate.

NGOs' mobilization for binding human rights norms in the EPAs, instead, found support in the European Commission. Despite resistance from African delegations (Sicurelli 2009), the tight enforcement measures included in the Cotonou Agreement with respect to human rights compelled the parties to include the broadest range of measures that they foresaw in cases of human rights violations ever included by the EU in trade agreements with low- and middle-income countries.

Table 4.2 Political-economy dynamics in the trade negotiations with the ACP states

	Interest group mobilization for market access	*Domino effect*	*GVCs*
EU–CARIFORUM negotiations	• Farmer organizations. • Development NGOs. • Services industry.	In 2005 the Dominican Republic concluded an FTA with the US and Central America (CAFTA-DR). Specific trade liberalization commitments between the EU and the Dominican Republic have been modelled upon that agreement.	Low integration of Caribbean countries in the GVCs.
EU–Sub-Saharan African states negotiations	• Farmer organizations. • Development NGOs.	No domino effect. ACP region mostly indirectly relevant for the EU's global trade agenda.	Low integration of Sub-Saharan African countries in the GVCs.

4.5 Conclusions

Due to the low integration of ACP countries in the GVCs and the lack of relevant domino effects associated with other PTAs, the negotiations for the EPAs mobilized especially European farmers' organizations and NGOs. Service industries exceptionally represented an import-dependent sector that mobilized, especially in the negotiations with CARIFORUM.

The wide mobilization of European and African NGOs, coupled with the lack of European offensive interests, resulted in substantial concessions from the EU to its ACP partners, and especially the African delegations. As a result, the EPAs are the most development-friendly PTAs negotiated in the 2000s. The asymmetrical liberalization requirements and transition periods, the flexible rules of origin, and protection for infant industry in favour of ACP countries, coupled with the high standards of sustainable development and human rights clauses, seem to confirm the representation of the EU as a normative power in its relations with the ACP countries. Yet, the commercial interests were not absent in the shaping of the European negotiating position. More specifically, protectionist interest groups in the agricultural sector obtained exceptional protection in the EPAs. Finally, the service sector obtained an agreement with the CARIFORUM with strong service liberalization commitments.

Notes

1. The member countries of CARIFORUM are Antigua and Barbuda, Bahamas, Barbados, Belize, Dominica, the Dominican Republic, Grenada, Guyana, Jamaica, St Lucia, St Vincent and the Grenadines, St Kitts and Nevis, Suriname, and Trinidad and Tobago.
2. Benin, Burkina Faso, Cape Verde, Gambia, Ghana, Guinea, Guinea Bissau, Ivory Coast, Liberia, Mauritania, Mali, Niger, Nigeria, Senegal, Sierra Leone, and Togo.
3. SADC member countries are Botswana, Lesotho, Mozambique, Swaziland, Namibia, and South Africa. Even though South Africa is not a member of the ACP group and is not a party to the Cotonou Agreement, it is a party to the agreement as a member of SADC. The EPA with SADC has replaced the EU–South Africa Trade, Development and Cooperation Agreement signed in 1999.
4. EAC members are Burundi, Kenya, Rwanda, Tanzania, and Uganda.
5. Interview, ACP Secretariat, Brussels, 27 September 2008.
6. Interview, DG Trade, Brussels, 20 June, 2017.

7. Interview, DG Trade, Brussels, 24 September 2008.
8. Interview, DG Trade, Brussels, 20 June 2017.
9. Interview, DG Trade, Brussels, 24 September 2008.
10. Interview, ETUC, Brussels, 27 May 2014.
11. Interview, DG Trade, Brussels, 20 June 2017.
12. Interview, DG Trade, Brussels, 20 June 2017.
13. Interview, DG Trade, Brussels, 20 June 2017.
14. Interview, DG Development, Brussels, 16 September 2008.
15. Interview, ETUC, 27 May 2014.

References

Agritrade. 2007. *EU Farmers' Reaction to Revised EC Proposals.* Press Release, 13 August.

Alter and Meunier. 2006.

Bilal S., and I. Ramdoo. 2016. Sustainability and Human Rights in EPAs. A Comparative Analysis Between the Caribbean and African EPAs. Discussion Paper, 198. European Centre for Development Policy Management. September. https://www.researchgate.net/profile/Sanoussi_Bilal/publication/308160463_Sustainability_and_human_rights_in_EPAs_A_comparative_analysis_between_the_Caribbean_and_African_EPAs/links/57db964c08ae5292a376b2d2.pdf.

Borrmann, A., and M. Busse. 2007. The Institutional Challenge of the ACP/EU Economic Partnership Agreements. *Development Policy Review* 25 (4): 403–416.

Brundsen, J. 2008. EPAs Pose Threat to ACP Regional Integration. *European Voice,* 18 March.

Byron, J., and P. Levis. 2007. *Formulating Sustainable Development Benchmarks for an EU-CARIFORUM EPA: Caribbean Perspectives.* Report Prepared for the International Centre for Trade and Sustainable Development and the Association of World Council of Churches related Development Organizations in Europe.

Center for International Environmental Law. 2008. *Intellectual Property in European Union Economic Partnership Agreements with the African, Caribbean and Pacific Countries: What Way Forward After the CARIFORUM EPA and the Interim EPAs?* Policy Report.

Commission of the African Union and the Economic Commission for Africa. 2007. Short Background Brief on Economic Partnership Agreements.

Daugbjerg, C., and A. Swinbank. 2008. Curbing Agricultural Exceptionalism: The EU's Response to External Challenge. *World Economy* 31 (5): 631–652.

Deckwirth, C. 2005. *The EU Corporate Trade Agenda: The Role and the Interests of Corporations and Their Lobby Groups in Trade Policy-Making in the European Union.* Policy Paper, Brussels/Berlin (November).

Dür, A., and D. De Bièvre. 2007. Inclusion Without Influence: NGOs in European Trade Policy. *Journal of Public Policy* 27 (1): 79–101.

Euractiv. 2008. EU-Africa Economic Partnership Agreements: Opportunity or Car Crash? Brussels, 11 January.

Eurocommerce. 2007. *Preferential Rules of Origin. Comments on the Proposed Reform*. Position Paper, Brussels.

European Commission. 2006. *Global Europe: Competing in the World*. COM (2006) 567 Final, 4 October.

———. 2008. Caribbean Region—Regional Strategy Paper and Regional Indicative Programme, 2008–2013. Strasbourg, November 15.

———. 2010. *The Public Consultation on the Future EU Trade Policy: Overview of Contributions*. Report. http://trade.ec.europa.eu/doclib/docs/2010/september/tradoc_146556.pdf.

———. 2011. Civil Society Dialogue Meeting on Economic Partnership Agreements (EPAs) and on the Review of the Generalised System of Preferences (GSP) Regulation. http://trade.ec.europa.eu/doclib/docs/2011/june/tradoc_147962.pdf.

———. 2012. *Economic Partnership Agreements (EPAs): State of Play*. Meeting, Brussles, February. http://trade.ec.europa.eu/civilsoc/meetdetails.cfm?meet=11382.

Europeanmilkboard. 2016. *Europe's Dairy Sector Has Its Eyes on West Africa, June*. Report. http://www.europeanmilkboard.org/fileadmin/Dokumente/Newsletter/2016/EtudIndusLait-EN-Web.pdf.

Faber, G., and J. Orbie. 2007. The EU's Insistence On Reciprocal Trade With The ACP Group. Economic Interests in the Driving Seat? In *Beyond Market Access for Economic Development: EU-Africa relations in Transition*, ed. G. Faber and J. Orbie, 38–64. London and New York: Routledge.

Flint, A. 2009. The End of a 'Special Relationship'? The New EU-ACP Economic Partnership Agreements. *Review of African Political Economy* 119: 79–92.

FOE 2006. *Corporate Conquest. Why the UK and Its EU Partners Must Stop Forcing Economic Partnership Agreements (EPAs) Upon Developing Countries*. Report, September. https://www.foe.co.uk/sites/default/files/downloads/corporate_conquest.pdf.

Gammage, C. 2017. *North-South Regional Trade Agreements as Legal Regimes. A Critical Assessment of the EU-SADC Economic Partnership Agreement*. Cheltenham: Edward Elgar.

Girvan, N. 2010. Technification, Sweetification, Treatyfication: Politics of the Caribbean-EU Economicpartnership Agreement. *Interventions* 12 (1): 100–111.

Heron, T. 2011. Asymmetric Bargaining and Development Trade-Offs in the CARIFORUM-European Union Economic Partnership Agreement. *Review of International Political Economy* 18 (3): 328–357.

Heron, T., and P. Murray-Evans. 2017. Limits to Market Power: Strategic Discourse and Institutional Path Dependence in the European Union-African, Caribbean and Pacific Economic Partnership Agreements. *European Journal of International Relations* 23 (2): 341–364.

Heron, T., and G. Siles-Brügge. 2012. Competitive Liberalization and the 'Global Europe' Services and Investment Agenda: Locating the Commercial Drivers of the EU–ACP Economic Partnership Agreements. *Journal of Common Market Studies* 50 (2): 250–266.

Kategekwa, J. 2013. *Opening Markets for Foreign Skills: How Can the WTO Help?* London: Springer.

Kerremans, B., and M.M. Gistelinck. 2009. Labour Rights in EPAs: Can the EU-CARIFORUM EPA Be a Guide? In *Beyond Market Access for Development: EU-Africa Relations in Transition*, ed. G. Faber and J. Orbie, 304–321. London and New York: Routledge.

LaForce, V.C. 2014. The EU-Caribbean Trade Relationship Post-Lisbon: The Case of Bananas. *Journal of Contemporary European Research* 10 (2): 66–279.

Langan, M. 2014. Decent Work and Indecent Trade Agendas: The European Union and ACP Countries. *Contemporary Politics* 20 (1): 23–35.

Montoute, A. 2016. Deliberate or Emancipate? Civil Society Participation in Trade Policy: The Case of the CARIFORUM–EU EPA. *International Journal of Voluntary and Nonprofit Organizations* 27 (1): 299–321.

Nord, R. 2015. Global Value Chains: The Missing Link in Sub-Saharan Africa's Trade Integration. Blog Ideas for Development: *Agence française de développement*, 13 July. http://ideas4development.org/en/global-value-chains-the-missing-link-in-sub-saharan-africas-trade-integration/.

Nyaga Munyi, E. 2016. Beyond Asymmetry: Substantive Beliefs in Preference Formation and Efficiency of Asymmetrical Negotiations. *New Political Economy* 21 (1): 49–68.

Oxfam. 2005. *Making Trade Work for Development in 2005: What the EU Should Do*. Briefing Paper, May.

———. 2006. *Unequal Partners: How EU–ACP Economic Partnership Agreements (EPAs) Could Harm the Development Prospects of Many of the World's Poorest Countries*. Briefing Note, September. https://www.oxfam.org/sites/www.oxfam.org/files/unequal%20partners.pdf.

———. 2008. *Partnership or Power Play? How Europe Should Bring Development into Its Trade Deals with African, Caribbean, and Pacific countries*. Briefing Paper.

Poletti, A. 2012. *The European Union and Multilateral Trade Governance: The Politics of the Doha Round*. London: Routledge.

Poletti, A., and D. De Bièvre. 2014. Political Mobilization, Veto Players, and WTO Litigation: Explaining European Union Responses in Trade Disputes. *Journal of European Public Policy* 21 (8): 1181–1198.

Robinson, D., and C. Gibson. 2011. Governing Knowledge: Discourses and Tactics of the European Union in Trade-Related Intellectual Property Negotiations. *Antipode* 43 (5): 1883–1910.

Sauvé, P., and N. Ward. 2009. *The EC-CARIFORUM Economic Partnership Agreement: Assessing the Outcome on Services and Investment*. Report, European Center for International Political Economy, Brussels, January, 2009.

Sicurelli, D. 2010. *The European Union's Africa Policies. Norms, Interests and Impact*. Farnham and Burlington, VT: Ashgate.

Spence, M. 2009. *Negotiating Trade, Innovation and Intellectual Property: Lessons from the CARIFORUM EPA Experience from a Negotiator's Perspective*. UNCTAD, Policy Brief, N. 4, September. http://unctad.org/en/Docs/iprs_pb20094_en.pdf.

Stevens, C. 2008. Economic Partnership Agreements: What Can We Learn? *New Political Economy* 13 (2): 211–223.

Stop Epa. 2007. *Economic Partnership Agreements: Building or shattering African regional Integration?* Policy Report. http://www.stopepa.de/img/traidcraft_etal_building_or_shattering.pdf.

Suvye Phiri, D. 2009, Economic Partnership Agreements and Intellectual Property Rights Protection: Challenges for the Southern African Development Community Region, South African Institute of International Affairs, Occasional Paper 48, October.

Tempest, M. 2017. Merkel's 'Man in Africa' Downbeat on Prospects for Africa-EU Summit. Euractiv, 12 April.

The Economist. 2007. A Desperate Suitor. After China and America, It Is Europe's Turn to Woo Africa, 6 December.

Trommer, S. 2014. Legal Opportunity in Trade Negotiations: International Law, Opportunity Structures and the Political Economy of Trade Agreements. *New Political Economy* 19 (1): 1–20.

Vahl, R. 2011. From Cotonou to Bridgetown: The Birth of the Caribbean EPA. In *The CARIFORUM-EU Economic Partnership Agreement: A Practitioner Analysis*, eds. A. Beviglia Zampetti and J. Lodge, 1–10.

Weinhardt, C. 2014. The Recent EU-West Africa Trade Deal Is Not Everybody's Success Story. *Bridges Africa* 3 (3), 9 April. http://www.ictsd.org/bridges-news/bridges-africa/news/the-recent-eu-west-africa-trade-deal-is-not-everybody%E2%80%99s-success.

Woolcock, S.J. 2014. Differentiation Within Reciprocity: The European Union Approach to Preferential Trade Agreements. *Contemporary Politics* 20 (1): 36–48.

CHAPTER 5

Trade Agreements with ASEAN Countries

Abstract The position of the EU in the negotiations with Vietnam shows that the EU is less prone to concede long transition periods and flexible rules of origin to an ASEAN country than to Latin American countries. Moreover, the agreement includes a soft language concerning suspension of reciprocal trade commitments in case of human rights violations, while it promotes the most detailed consultation procedure in the enforcement of sustainable development. A comparison with the trade agreement concluded with Singapore also shows that the EU has exerted greater pressures on Vietnam to adjust to EU regulatory standards than to other high-income ASEAN members. Due to the downstream location of Vietnam in high-tech manufacturing and to its labour-intensive industry, import-dependent and sector-specific protectionist groups strongly mobilized in order to affect the negotiations. Competition with the US also strengthened European exporters' interest to obtain conditions enabling access to these countries' markets similar to those granted to their US counterparts. NGOs found allies in the protectionist industry in the promotion of high labour and environmental standards and strict enforcement procedures. However, these groups proved less effective in pushing forward binding human rights clauses. Similar patterns of societal mobilization are emerging in the ongoing negotiations with other ASEAN members.

Keywords Vietnam • European exporter • import-dependent interests • import-competing firms • NGOs

A. Poletti, D. Sicurelli, *The Political Economy of Normative Trade Power Europe*, https://doi.org/10.1007/978-3-319-78864-7_5

5.1 Introduction

The internal heterogeneity of ASEAN, in terms of levels of development of its members, makes the region an interesting test for the differentiation approach adopted by the EU to link trade and development objectives. In South East Asia, the EU has so far concluded trade deals with Singapore (2014) and Vietnam (2015), and is currently negotiating preferential agreements with other members. Singapore is a small, high-income country and one of the wealthier countries in the world, while Vietnam is a lower-middle-income country, according to World Bank classifications. A comparison between the two agreements, though, shows that the negotiating position of the EU with regard to the two partners has been only marginally congruent with a strategy that formally aims to take into account the different developmental needs of trading partners. The following sections show that the EU has conceded a limited number of flexibility measures to Vietnam, aimed at supporting the efforts of the country to adjust to liberalization requirements included in the deal, but also that those measures are not proportional to the relatively high costs of adjustment to the trade agreement imposed on Vietnam in comparison to Singapore. Most notably, the EU has conceded fewer flexibility measures to Vietnam than it did to its Latin American trade partners.

Political-economy dynamics contributed to the shaping of the EU position for this trade agreement with Vietnam. The domino effect triggered by negotiations concerning the Trans Pacific Partnership (TPP) and the EU–Singapore agreement, as well as the high integration of Vietnam in GVCs, has affected the organized societal interests of Europe and ultimately harmed the coherence of European trade policy relations with Vietnam in respect of the EU self-declared normative goals. More specifically, pressure from importers, exporters, and investors for trade liberalization and regulatory harmonization has prevailed over the concern of NGOs for a development-friendly deal and for binding human rights clauses. At the same time, as a reaction to an alliance between protectionist interests and NGOs for the promotion of high sustainability standards, the EU–Vietnam FTA imposes tighter regulatory standards in the field of labour protection than the agreement with Singapore.

This chapter is structured as follows. The first part offers an overview of the negotiations between the EU and ASEAN countries, which started in 2007 and ended in a failure in 2009, in order to provide some background information on the obstacles that characterized these inter-regional negotiations and the context within which the EU decided to proceed with bilateral trade negotiations. The second part analyses the text of the FTA with Vietnam (2015), contrasting it with the provisions of the EU–Singapore (2014) trade agreement in order to assess whether the EU did indeed pursue a differentiated approach as declared in the Commission's Communication on Trade, Growth, and Development (2012). The third part focuses on the process that has led to the negotiating position of the EU in the bilateral negotiations with Vietnam (2012–2015), tracing the impact of lobbying by European business interest groups and pressure from NGOs. Finally, it discusses the role of major interest groups mobilized in reaction to the ongoing trade negotiations with Malaysia, Indonesia, and the Philippines. The conclusions discuss the implications of the PTAs signed by the EU with South East Asian members for ASEAN economic integration and development cooperation in the region.

5.2 Negotiations with ASEAN (2007–2009)

The domino effect triggered by trade negotiations between ASEAN and major trade powers has clearly contributed to the mobilization of European stakeholders interested in developing trade relations with ASEAN members. The high integration of those economies in GVCs, furthermore, influenced the mobilization patterns of EU stakeholders.

The EU first considered negotiating a trade agreement with ASEAN in 2002. In the same year, Singapore and Japan had signed the 'new age' EPA, and ASEAN as a whole had concluded a trade deal with China and had started trade negotiations with the US within the framework of the Enterprise for ASEAN Initiative. Those agreements inevitably triggered a reaction in the EU, at the time still a relatively marginal player in the region (Garcìa 2013; Meissner 2016; Sahakyan 2016).

In 2005, a Vision Group on ASEAN–EU Economic Partnership was established in order to examine the feasibility of a possible ASEAN–EU Free Trade Area. The Report of the Vision Group promoted a trade agreement that would take into account the development needs of the developing Asian members. It called for an inter-regional agreement, which would promote a 'mixture of liberalization and cooperation between economies of different levels of development'. More specifically, 'the less developed economies should be granted longer transition periods, allowing for a more gradual phasing-in of their commitments' and cooperation between economies of different levels of development. The Report was thus considered to have explicitly introduced the concept of differentiation, that is, the idea that trade policy should be differentiated according to the development needs of trade partners.

This important idea, however, was not reflected in the strategic framework for trade policy laid out shortly afterwards by the European Commission in its Communication 'Global Europe: Competing in the World' (2006). Indeed, the Communication mainly emphasized the purpose of contributing to growth and jobs in Europe through trade agreements, without explicitly mentioning the need to take into account the different development needs of trading partners. As far as Asia is concerned, the document observed that 'European exports are strong in countries where demand is static but they are less well placed than Japan and the US in rapidly growing markets, particularly in Asia', and 'while our current bilateral agreements support our neighborhood and development objectives well, our main trade interests, including in Asia, are less well served'.

As a result of the Global Europe Communication, the EU launched negotiations with a number of Asian partners, namely, the ASEAN countries, India, and South Korea. Based on the size of the Indian and ASEAN markets and on the economic power of South Korea, the Commission identified heightened market potential in negotiations with those partners (Gavin and Sindzingre 2009). Region-to-region negotiations with ASEAN countries started in 2007. After slow progress, though, the two parties declared an end to negotiations in 2009, when inter-regional divergences and, especially, divisions between ASEAN countries made it clear that a successful conclusion to these negotiations was not at hand.

Even though EU negotiators declared that divergences between the two regions on human rights violations in Myanmar were the major cause of the stalemate, ASEAN's lack of capacity to act as a unitary player ultimately prevented the conclusion of an inter-regional deal. European negotiators claimed that ASEAN's refusal to exclude Myanmar from the agreement, due to EU criticism of the human rights record of its military dictatorship and its repression of pro-democracy groups, was the major cause of disagreement between the two parties. For instance, in August

2007 the former High Representative for Common Foreign and Security Policy, Javier Solana, asked that Myanmar, due to human rights violations, should not be included in the inter-regional trade deal (Doan 2012). In the EU–ASEAN summit of November 2007, though, the EU foreign ministers appeared more flexible on the topic and agreed that Myanmar would not be excluded from trade talks (Euractiv 2007). Despite agreement on this issue, the complex set of issues under negotiation, and the diverse composition of ASEAN members in terms of levels and models development, made it impossible for countries in the region to agree on a common negotiating position with the EU.[1] A lack of political will from ASEAN governments (European Parliament 2008) represented a further insurmountable obstacle to the conclusion of the agreement. As a result, the EU decided to start negotiating bilaterally with individual ASEAN members, a decision that was officially meant to create building blocks for a future region-to-region deal, but in practice put an end to the idea of pursuing an inter-regional trade strategy with ASEAN countries.

Singapore was the first ASEAN partner to negotiate a bilateral trade agreement with the EU early in 2010. As the Commission (2009) explained, 'With around €55 billion of bilateral trade, Singapore is the EU's most important trading partner in the region'. The small and wealthy city-state is also the biggest investment partner of the EU among the ASEAN countries. In selecting Singapore as the first ASEAN partner for negotiating a bilateral deal, the EU also followed the US example, which had concluded a trade agreement with Singapore in 2014. Both the US and the EU considered Singapore as a benchmark for future bilateral agreements with the region. According to the Commission (2009), while starting negotiations with Singapore, 'the door remains open for other ASEAN countries willing to negotiate a comprehensive trade agreement with the EU'. In 2015, the EU concluded a trade agreement with Vietnam.

5.3 The EU–Vietnam Trade Agreement (2015)

While the Commission's Communication (2006) aimed at stimulating European exports in the region, import-dependent interests were the main actors that mobilized during the negotiations with ASEAN and single member states (Eckhardt and Poletti 2016). The relevance of ASEAN for European exporters and especially importers is evident in EU trade statistics for the region. As opposed to trade flows with Latin American and ACP countries (see Chaps. 3 and 4), since 2006 the EU has consistently had a negative balance of trade in goods with ASEAN (European Commission 2017). Thus, European import-dependent groups interested in further increasing their import opportunities from ASEAN had high stakes in these negotiations. The high integration of ASEAN economies in GVCs and the downstream ranking in the high-tech manufacturing and labour-intensive industry of most of its members have made the South East Asian market especially interesting for European importers. In contrast to trade in goods, as far as trade in services is concerned, the EU recorded a surplus from 2005 to 2012 (Eurostat 2015). In that sector, therefore, exporters had an interest in preserving their market share.

The trade agreement concluded by the EU with Vietnam 'is the most ambitious trade pact—both on market access and on rule-making—ever signed by the EU with a developing country' (Dreyer 2015). A comparison between trade agreements signed by the EU with Singapore and Vietnam clearly suggests that the EU has treated both countries quite similarly, despite huge differences in terms of their development needs. In fact, the following sections suggest that the EU successfully pushed forward an agenda that is largely similar to the one it pursued with developed countries such as Singapore (Table 5.1).

Table 5.1 The EU–Singapore and EU–Vietnam trade agreements

	EU-Singapore FTA	*EU-Vietnam FTA*
Market access to the EU	Tariff elimination in 5 years.	Tariff elimination in 7 years.
Market access to the partner	Tariff elimination in 5 years.	Tariff elimination in 10 years.
Anti-dumping	No infant industry protection clause. Standard reciprocal bilateral safeguard measures to protect domestic producers.	No infant industry protection clause. Standard reciprocal bilateral safeguard measures to protect domestic producers.
Rules of origin	ASEAN cumulation for key exports.	ASEAN cumulation for key exports. In the sector of textiles: double transformation rule. Cumulation with South Korea.

(*continued*)

Table 5.1 (continued)

	EU-Singapore FTA	*EU-Vietnam FTA*
Trade in service	WTO-plus liberalization of telecommunications, financial, computer, transport, postal, environmental sectors.	WTO-plus liberalization of telecommunications, financial, computer, transport, postal, environmental sectors.
Investment	ISDS, with no emphasis on state's right to regulate and no appeal mechanism.	Investment court system, with emphasis on state's right to regulate and with an appeal mechanism.
Government procurement	Confirming Singapore's commitments under the GPA.	Asking Vietnam to comply with GPA-compatible standards.
SOEs	• Detailed conditions to increase the competitiveness of SOEs and private enterprises. • Rules on transparency and consultations on domestic subsidies.	• Detailed conditions to increase the competitiveness of SOEs and private enterprises. • Rules on transparency and consultations on domestic subsidies.
Intellectual property rights	TRIPS-plus protection.	TRIPS-plus protection.
Sustainable development	• Calling for ratification and enforcement of all the core UN environmental and labour Conventions compatibly with 'domestic circumstances'. • Consultation of civil society and experts.	• Calling for ratification and enforcement of all the core UN environmental and labour conventions compatibly with 'domestic circumstances'. • Consultation of civil society and experts, with detailed procedures and conditions.
Human rights	• Institutional linkage with the Partnership and Cooperation Agreement (PCA). • Dialogue as an enforcement mechanism.	• Institutional linkage with the PCA. • Dialogue as an enforcement mechanism.

Note: PCA: Partnership and Cooperation Agreement

Vietnam has obtained more concessions than Singapore in the field of market access. On the one hand, the EU–Singapore trade agreement is fully reciprocal in terms of tariff elimination. The contracting parties have agreed to conclude the process in five years once the agreement has entered into force. On the other hand, the EU–Vietnam trade agreement requires Vietnam to liberalize 65% of import duties on EU exports at entry into force, and eliminate the remaining duties over a ten-year period. Vietnam also consented to lift most of its export duties, with few exceptions (pharmaceutics and motor vehicles). The EU, in turn, agreed on eliminating its export duties over seven years. The EU exempts rice and other agricultural products from full liberalization, but offers access to Vietnamese exports in those sectors via tariff rate quotas. Thus, even though access for Vietnamese products in these sectors of the European market remains limited, it is no longer totally restricted.

On anti-dumping, both agreements include reciprocal bilateral measures and, similarly to trade agreements concluded with Latin American countries, they do not include provisions to protect infant industries. Those measures, though, are especially sensitive in the case of Vietnam, which had been involved in anti-dumping disputes with the EU with respect to leather footwear between 2006 and 2011. In 2015 the EU launched an anti-dumping investigation on the same product, which led to the decision to reimpose anti-dumping duties on Vietnam.

The EU has promoted equivalent regulatory standards in the trade negotiations with the two ASEAN members. Both Singapore and Vietnam enjoy cumulation of rules of origin for a number of key exports with ASEAN members with which the EU has a trade agreement in force. Nevertheless, the specificity of the structure of Vietnam's economy makes those rules more restrictive for that country than for Singapore. While services mainly drive Singapore's external trade relations, Vietnam mainly exports goods, which are often the result of transformation of products imported from China and other trade partners.[2] Textiles, for example, are excluded from ASEAN cumulation. To benefit from preferential access, rules of origin in this sector impose the use fabrics produced in Vietnam, with the exception of fabrics produced in South Korea, which has already concluded a trade agreement with the EU. Moreover, the agreement imposes the double transformation rule (from fibre to fabric or from yarn to garment) to the sector of textiles, which requires fabrics to be woven or knitted in Vietnam to qualify for duty-free treatment. Most textiles made in Vietnam, though, are the result of transformation of inputs from China, which excludes them from preferential treatment.

Both trade agreements with Singapore and Vietnam provide the two parties with reciprocal liberalization commitments in the sector of services, including telecommunications, financial, computer, transport, business, environmental, postal and courier, banking, insurance, and maritime transport services. Thus, the trade deal with Vietnam pushes the country beyond its WTO commitments and the commitments it has undertaken in trade agreements with other partners (European Commission 2015).

In contrast to the trade agreements concluded by the EU with Latin American countries, deals concluded with ASEAN countries include an investment chapter. Negotiations with the former group of countries, as a matter of fact, had started before the Lisbon Treaty had entered into force. Therefore, the European Commission had no mandate to negotiate on this chapter. Vietnam, like Singapore, consented to liberalize investments in multiple sectors. Both agreements include an investor-state dispute settlement mechanism, even though the mechanism included in the EU–Vietnam deal differs from all ISDS's previously included in EU trade agreements in terms of the guarantees of protection it provides to the state vis-à-vis investors, namely, an appeal mechanism and an emphasis on the state's right to regulate.

On government procurement, the trade agreement with Vietnam imposes higher costs on the country than does that with Singapore. In contrast to Singapore, Vietnam is not a member of the GPA. While the agreement with Singapore merely confirms commitments already mutually accepted in the GPA, Vietnam is asked to fully accept disciplines it did not previously agree upon in the WTO framework. More specifically, the government procurement chapter allows EU investors to bid for public contracts with Vietnamese ministers, and Vietnam also agreed to liberalize bids concerning 34 public hospitals, state-owned enterprises (SOEs), and the 2 biggest cities, Hanoi and Ho Chi Minh City.

The provisions on SOEs also largely mirror those included in the trade agreement with Singapore. Both agreements legitimize public undertakings and monopolies, but ask contracting states to remove subsidies for ailing or insolvent undertakings that have disruptive effects on trade between the parties. They also establish the conditions for the competitiveness of SOEs and private enterprises, and rules on transparency and consultation on state subsidies. These measures make the chapter more ambitious and binding than the restrictions on SOEs included in any other trade agreement concluded by Vietnam.

The two deals also include rules concerning IPR which extend commitments that Singapore and Vietnam had undertaken under the TRIPS. Following the models of trade deals concluded with Latin American countries, they also specify that the two states should adopt the European approach to geographical indications.

The sustainable development chapters in the two agreements call on the parties to implement the ILO Conventions and multilateral environmental treaties which they have ratified and to ratify the other conventions and treaties. In contrast to trade agreements concluded with Latin American countries and with ACP countries, though, the trade deals with Singapore and Vietnam specify that the contracting parties will consider ratifying

ILO conventions taking into account their 'domestic circumstances'. Quite surprisingly, the chapter includes provisions which are more binding, and thus impose greater adjustment costs, for Vietnam than for Singapore. As far as ILO standards are concerned, for instance, Singapore has ratified six out of the eight fundamental ILO Conventions, but Vietnam only five.[3] Above all, Vietnam's Constitution does not recognize the freedom of association, and trade unions in Vietnam can only be established legally under the umbrella of the Vietnam General Confederation of Labour, which is under the control of the Communist Party. Furthermore, the mechanisms for monitoring the enforcement of the chapter in the EU–Vietnam deal are more rigid than those included in the EU–Singapore agreement. The former requires that a specialized committee on trade and sustainable development shall meet within the first year after the agreement enters into force, and thereafter as necessary. The committee needs to review the implementation of specific cooperation activities listed in Article 12. Such a list is absent in the agreement with Singapore.

Finally, the two agreements include identical human rights clauses. They tie the trade agreement with the Partnership and Cooperation Agreements concluded by the two countries (Vietnam in 2012 and Singapore in 2013). In contrast to agreements with the CARIFORUM, however, the Partnership and Cooperation Agreements with the two Asian countries do not make explicit reference to the possibility of suspending reciprocal trade commitments as a reaction to human rights violations in one of the contracting parties. In contrast to the Cotonou Agreement, furthermore, the two Partnership and Cooperation Agreements do not require that political dialogue should precede the consultation procedure in non-urgent cases.

5.4 Tracing EU Preferences in Negotiations with Asian Countries

Developing an explanation of the EU's decision to negotiate trade-liberalizing agreements with ASEAN countries in general, and with Vietnam in particular, based on the interests of domestic business seems difficult at first glance. Indeed, standard political-economy explanations of trade policy seem to suggest that liberalizing trade between countries with different levels of economic developments should be difficult to achieve politically (Manger 2012). For one thing, these agreements can be expected to generate significant negative distributive effects for capital-abundant countries because their least competitive sectors become exposed to imports from labour-abundant countries. At the same time, countries with low per capita incomes can be expected to represent relatively uninteresting markets for exporters of goods produced in high-cost locations (Eckahrdt and Poletti 2016). Thus, according to standard accounts viewing trade policy as the result of the conflict between exporters and import-competing groups, it is difficult to explain why negotiations between the EU and Asian countries with relatively low levels of economic development (such as Vietnam) have materialized, let alone successfully concluded.

As we elaborate in the following sections, focusing on the preferences, patterns of political action, and influence of European import-dependent firms can help to explain this apparent paradox. As explained in Chap. 1, we define import-dependent firms as firms that rely on the income generated by imported goods or on the import of intermediate products for their production process (Eckardt 2015). These actors, who have become more and more important in the context of an international economy increasingly organized around GVCs, have a strong preference for trade liberalization because it leads to a reduction in variable costs of their imports. Thus, a political-economy explanation of trade policy cannot neglect the political role of this set of increasingly important domestic firms. In the following sections, we develop such an explanation, showing how the EU trade policy strategy towards Asian countries was also crucially affected by import-dependent firms, and therefore evolved as a result of their interplay with other traditionally influential actors such as exporters and import-competing groups. We start with a brief examination of the politics underlying negotiations with ASEAN countries in the 2007–2009 period. We then analyse in greater detail the political dynamics that characterized trade negotiations between the EU and Vietnam. Finally, we briefly look into ongoing trade negotiations between the EU and other Asian countries.

5.4.1 *The Politics of EU Negotiations with ASEAN*

While the Commission's Communication (2006) emphasized the potential for new EU trade agreements with ASEAN countries to stimulate European exports, it is important to mention that exporters were not the only domestic producers favouring this important trade initiative. In addition to exporters, import-dependent firms played a key political role in support of the Global Europe initiative (Eckhardt and Poletti 2016). For instance, our interviewees confirm that Eurocommerce, the organization representing the interests of the European retail and wholesale sectors, actively pushed from the very beginning for the signing of PTAs with ASEAN countries, lobbying the Commission and the European Parliament, while leaving it to national associations to exert pressure on national governments.[4] Such political activism is further witnessed by official position papers and documents released by the organization, expressing support for these trade initiatives, with particular emphasis on the need to reduce tariff and non-tariff barriers applied on ASEAN countries' imports (Eurocommerce 2007a, b, 2009). Similar views have also been expressed consistently by the Foreign Trade Association (2009), the other organization representing the interests of European import-dependent firms.[5]

Import-dependent firms thus added to the political weight of business organizations traditionally representing exporters' interests in Europe, which also supported this trade initiative. For instance, BusinessEurope and the European Services Forum expressed their support very early and pushed for the Global Europe communication, strongly advocating the opening of trade negotiations with ASEAN countries, and working closely with European Commission officials to define the negotiating agenda (BusinessEurope 2006, 2007a, b; European Services Forum 2006, 2007). As noted in the analysis of these policy positions carried out by Eckhardt and Poletti (2016), these organizations' support was motivated both by a need to access new markets and also by a desire to enable EU manufacturers to access cheaper imports in the context of supply-chain integration with ASEAN countries.

These positions are not surprising when one considers trade statistics between the EU and ASEAN countries in the period when the Global Europe initiative was launched. As opposed to trade flows with Latin American and ACP countries (see Chaps. 3 and 4), since 2006 the EU has steadily registered a negative balance of trade in goods with ASEAN countries (European Commission 2017). Thus, European import-dependent groups interested in further increasing their import opportunities from ASEAN countries have the greatest stake in the negotiations. The high level of participation of ASEAN economies in GVCs and the downstream ranking in the high-tech manufacturing and labour-intensive industry of most of its members have made the South East Asian market especially interesting for European importers. In contrast to trade in goods, from 2005 to 2012 the EU recorded a surplus in trade in services with the region (Eurostat 2015). In that sector, therefore, exporters had an interest in preserving and even increasing their market share.

5.4.2 *The Politics of EU–Vietnam Trade Negotiations*

Negotiations with Vietnam mainly mobilized import-dependent interest groups attracted by the country's price-competitive products. This is not surprising. Data on bilateral trade flows between the EU and Vietnam in the period preceding and during negotiations shows that EU import-dependent firms had high stakes in pushing for a trade-liberalizing agreement that would allow them to access imports more cheaply. For instance, Vertical Intra Industry Trade, an indirect measure of trade affecting import-dependent manufacturers, increased dramatically in the period before the beginning of bilateral trade negotiations. Also, 85% of total EU imports from Vietnam fall within sectors—food and beverages, footwear and textiles—which are typical products imported by retailers (for details on this data, see Eckhardt and Poletti 2016). Exporters and investors also voiced their interest in protecting their market share from other expanding trade partnerships with Vietnam (especially that with the US) and increasing their relations with the country and ASEAN more generally. The trade deal also partially accommodated demands of import-competing groups, especially in the sectors of rice, footwear, and textiles. Also, NGOs actively mobilized during the negotiations, due to concerns about the low labour costs behind Vietnam products and the lack of independence of its trade unions, and were able to obtain stricter sustainability provisions than those included in the EU–Singapore deal. Table 5.2 synthetizes the political-economy dynamics registered in the negotiations between the EU and ASEAN, on the one hand, and between the EU and Vietnam, on the other.

The interest of the government of Vietnam in increasing the autonomy of its national economy from China and in concluding negotiations with the EU before the 12th National Congress of the Communist Party strengthened the bargaining power of the EU. Also, a gap in the negotiation capacity of the Vietnamese delegation contributed to the unbalanced relationship between the two partners. As Mauro Petriccione, the EU Commission's negotiator, explained, 'They have—and I know as a matter of fact—a capacity problem, the Vietnamese negotiating team is very badly stretched', but they are committed to conclude negotiations with the US and the EU at the same time (Borderlex 2015).

The following sections of this chapter trace the impact of European interest groups and NGOs's demands on single chapters of the trade agreement.

5.4.2.1 *Market Access, Rules of Origin, and Anti-dumping*

Imports from Vietnam to the EU member states steadily increased from 2005 (€5.59 billion) to 2015 (when they reached €29.98 billion) and made the EU the main destination of Vietnamese exports in goods. In contrast, EU exports to Vietnam are more modest. They amounted to €1.9 billion in 2005, and to €8.54 billion ten years later. Vietnam's downstream ranking in high-tech manufacturing and its cheap labour market have made its products especially attractive for European retailers and import-dependent firms (Eckhardt and Poletti 2016). According to Eurocommerce (2007a), the European retail and wholesale sector was interested in facilitating imports from Vietnam, and it was especially interested in liberalizing trade in fresh and canned fruit, canned vegetables, cashew nuts, black pepper, frozen shrimps and tiger prawns, plastic bags, and textiles and garments. During the negotiations, the association pushed for lowering European trade and regulatory barriers to Vietnamese goods and including flexible rules of origin in the trade deal (Eurocommerce 2009, 2010, 2012). The Foreign trade Association (2012) expressed similar views, considering the liberalization of trade with Vietnam a top priority for European retailers, wholesalers, importers, and brand companies. It is worth mentioning that, in order to increase their political leverage, Eurocommerce and Foreign Trade Association created stable mechanisms of coordination in order to get a coherent message across to the relevant decision-makers (Eckahrdt and Poletti 2016). As European Commission officials themselves acknowledge, these political pressures significantly affected the EU's negotiating position.[6]

In turn, from a Vietnamese perspective, preserving a positive trade balance with the EU was instrumental in balancing the country's trade deficit with China and South Korea.[7] Under these conditions, importers appeared to have tangible influence on the final deal. The impact of European importers on the trade agreement with Vietnam is evident, for instance, in the high reciprocity of the tariff liberalization schedules from both sides, as compared to schedules agreed with any other developing nation. In this respect, during the negotiations the delegate of DG trade commented that the high degree of reciprocity obtained from Vietnam is 'a first in our relations with a developing country' (Borderlex 2015).

On the opposite front, European import-competing groups in specific sectors, especially in the textile, rice, and fishery sectors (Euratex 2010; Riso Italiano 2015; Eurothon 2012), likewise mobilized in defence of their protectionist interests. Despite resistance of the Vietnamese delegation, they contributed to the shape of the final deal. They obtained a larger transition period to lift trade barriers to Vietnamese products (seven years) as compared to the period included in the EU–Singapore trade agreement (five years), and the inclusion of the definition of rice and sugar as sensitive sectors in the agreement, though they had to accept concessions to Vietnam's exports of those products by offering exports via tariff rate quotas (Euractiv 2015). In the words of the EU Commission negotiator speaking at a European Parliament's hearing, without those concessions, 'one would have to wonder what is the interest of Vietnam in actually concluding the agreement' (Borderlex 2015).

The negotiating position of the EU on rules of origin represents a compromise between protectionist and import-dependent interests. The proposal to cumulate rules of origin with Korea is coherent with import-dependent and exporter companies (Eurocommerce 2007a) interested in promoting simple and harmonized rules. Euratex, in turn, obtained a special status of the textiles sector arguing that Vietnam had already agreed upon stricter rules of origin concerning textiles in the negotiations with the US. The yarn forward rule in the TPP, as a matter of fact, requires textile producers in its member states to use yarn produced in TPP countries in order to receive duty-free access. In reaction to Euratex' pressure, and in contrast to Eurocommerce (2015)'s position, the European Commission imposed the exclusion of textiles from ASEAN cumulation, though it conceded cumulation with South Korea in relation to fabrics, and accepted the double transformation rule. Double transformation, more specifically, was a victory for Euratex against Eurocommerce's pressure for the single transformation rule (2015), which would facilitate imports in Europe.

The tension between European importers and import-competing groups in the shaping of the European Commission proposal was also evident in the footwear sector, where both types of interests are represented. The Foreign Trade Association, which represents import-dependent firms, namely, footwear makers sourcing inputs from foreign producers, promoted reciprocal liberalization commitments (Eckardt 2011), arguing 'there is no European manufacturer of the type of low cost shoes that are being imported from China and Vietnam' (Mallinder 2008). In order to address their demands, and in line with the Foreign Trade Association (2012)'s official position paper, footwear was not considered a sensitive sector in the trade agreement.[8] However, import-competing manufacturers from Italy, Portugal, and Spain, represented by the Confederation of the Footwear Industry, obtained the concession that no clause constraining the ability to resort to the imposition of anti-dumping measures against infant industries be included in the agreement.[9]

5.4.2.2 Trade in Services, Investments, Public Procurement, and SOEs
Exporters in the services sector and investors both considered the trade agreement with Vietnam a crucial deal, especially because it was expected to be a model for the future agreement with ASEAN members. In contrast to Singapore, the structure of Vietnam's economy is more similar to that of the other ASEAN members.[10] Despite the EU Commission negotiators having acknowledged that achieving greater commitment from Vietnam to service liberalization than that which followed its entry into the WTO in 2007 'is not easy' (Borderlex 2015), exporters in the service sectors (mainly insurance and banking sector companies) expected to benefit from the agreement (Dreyer 2015). The chapter of the agreement concerning service in trade shows that their pressure had an impact upon the Commission's position, which promoted an agreement aimed at liberalizing a broad range of services. Building upon the model of the EU–Singapore agreement, Vietnam has agreed to liberalize trade in financial services, telecommunications, transport, postal, and courier services.

Above all, the major winners among European service providers include pharmaceutical and other medical services providers. They are expected to particularly benefit from the provisions included in the government procurement chapter, which will allow them to bid for contracts in Vietnamese hospitals (Dreyer 2015). This result is especially remarkable, given the strong initial resistance of the Vietnamese delegation to deep liberalization commitments in this sector (Borderlex 2015). In this respect, the EU was able to obtain a deeper commitment on government procurement than the US in the context of the TPP or any other trade partner of Vietnam. The public procurement chapter also includes deeper liberalization commitments than those included in the trade agreements with Colombia, Peru, and CA (see Chap. 3). In short, European companies achieved 'a degree of transparency and procedural fairness comparable to other EU FTAs with developed countries' (European Commission 2015).

Another highly controversial topic in the negotiations was the discipline of SOEs (Sicurelli 2015a). In the words of the EU trade negotiator Petriccione, reaching an agreement on SOEs in this case was 'predictably complex' (Borderlex 2015). While the government considers Vietnam a 'socialist-oriented market economy' (Hoang 2016), the country has not yet obtained the status of a market economy in the context of the WTO, precisely due to the high role of the state in the economy. Given these structural constraints, the Vietnamese delegation made clear that it would not accept a deal that binds the government to liberalization of SOEs.[11]

Yet, it ultimately accepted detailed conditions that would create fair competition between SOEs and private enterprises. The agreement concluded with Vietnam was built upon the model of the EU–Singapore FTA and the precedent of the TPP.

European investors also considered Vietnam an increasingly attractive target. In 2015, in fact, the EU became the major non-Asian investment partner of the country (EU Delegation to Vietnam 2016). The Vietnam delegation was eager to conclude an agreement on the investment chapter, since, by being the first developing member of ASEAN to have concluded both the TPP and the FTA negotiations with the EU, it expected to enjoy a first-mover advantage as investment target for regional supply chains. Thus, the investment chapter included in the agreement can be considered a success both for European investors in key sectors such as healthcare and for Vietnam, which aims at becoming an investment hub in ASEAN (Dreyer 2015).

Finally, negotiations on an investor-state dispute mechanism during the negotiations with Vietnam raised societal mobilization in the EU. Despite pressure from European investors and the will of the Vietnamese government to achieve an ambitious deal in this sector, NGO criticism of the inclusion of this type of mechanism in the parallel negotiations for a TTIP found large support in a group of EU member states, especially Germany, Austria, and France. These protests also affected negotiations with Vietnam. In order to address those concerns, the Commission proposed a new model of dispute mechanism, namely, an investment court, which includes an appeal mechanism and explicitly stresses the state's right to regulate. This mechanism is expected to be a model for future trade agreements and a first step towards the long-term project of promoting a multilateral investment court.

5.4.2.3 *IPR, Sustainable Development, and Human Rights*

On IPR, the negotiating position of the EU contrasted with that of the US, especially due to their different approach to geographical indicators. Whereas the US's trade agreements consider geographical indications a chapter of trademark law, the EU promotes a sui generis system for the protection of geographical indications. 'Parmigiano Reggiano' (Parmesan), for instance, is considered a generic product in the US, while it is protected by EU law. According to the representative of the Vietnam Chamber of Commerce and Investment, Vietnam has chosen to follow the EU approach to geographical indications.[12] On this basis, it has negotiated an agreement with the US under the TPP that is compatible with this approach.

More controversial topics in the negotiations include sustainable development and human rights provisions (Sicurelli 2015a; Hoang 2016). Vietnam's Head of Mission to the EU, Ambassador Vuong Thua Phong, told members of the European Parliament that 'while encouraging high levels of protection, it is important that each party has the right to establish its own level of domestic environmental and labour protection' (Borderlex 2015). In a position paper on EU–ASEAN negotiations, Eurocommerce (2007a) claimed that 'trade policy should not be linked with social or environmental standards'. Yet, a coalition of European development NGOs, trade unions, and protectionist industries concerned about the implications of the labour-intensive export industries in Vietnam, both for domestic workers and for the competitiveness of European producers aimed at upholding high sustainability standards, was able to obtain more detailed enforcement rules than those included in the EU–Singapore deal in the chapter on sustainable development (Sicurelli 2015b; Hoang and Sicurelli 2017).

Negotiations about the inclusion of a human rights clause in the trade agreement, while failing to mobilize industry associations, again mobilized NGOs under the umbrella of the FIDH (2013). Even though the European Parliament (2009, 2014) voiced their demands for binding human rights standards in the agreement, and for the conclusion of an impact assessment on the human rights implications of the trade agreement before the conclusion of the negotiation, the lack of interest from European industry associations on this issue and the absence of human rights clauses in the TPP ultimately weakened those pressures. As a result, the trade agreement does include an institutional mechanism that ties the trade agreement with the Partnership and Cooperation Agreement between the two parties. In contrast to the FIDH and European Parliament's demands, though, the European Commission did not carry out a human rights impact assessment on the trade agreement. This decision was judged a case of maladministration by the European Ombudsman on February 2016.

5.4.3 *The Politics of Ongoing Negotiations with Other ASEAN States*

At the time of writing, the EU is negotiating bilateral trade agreements with other ASEAN members, including Malaysia, Indonesia, Myanmar, the Philippines, and Thailand. Like Vietnam, the Philippines and Indonesia belong to the group of lower-middle-income countries, according to the World Bank classification. Myanmar graduated from a least developed to lower-middle-income country in 2015, while Malaysia and Thailand are listed as upper-middle-income countries. Despite these differences, the mobilization patterns of European interest groups for these negotiations are similar to those registered in the negotiations with Vietnam. These ASEAN members share a similar economic structure, due to their high levels of integration in regional and GVCs. In contrast to the AC, CA, and ACP countries (see Chaps. 3 and 4), which predominantly export primary products, ASEAN members mainly export transformed products, such as electronics, transport equipment, and textiles. Furthermore, these are labour-intensive economies, which makes them especially attractive for European retailers. For these reasons, negotiations with the other ASEAN members so far have mainly mobilized import-dependent interests and, more marginally, import-competing groups. European industries have also expressed growing interest in the export and investment opportunities offered by the dynamic region of South East Asia.

Retailer associations participated extensively in the Commission's consultations on the shaping of a negotiating position for the trade deals with ASEAN members. In particular, Eurocommerce (2013) and the Foreign Trade Association (2014, 2015) encouraged the conclusion of FTAs with Thailand, the Philippines, and Myanmar, in order to facilitate the import of electronics, garments, textiles, footwear, processed fruit, coconut oil, and fish from those countries. To this end, those associations promoted duty-free access of those goods to the EU and simple and predictable rules of origin in the agreements. In turn, the European Services Forum (2011, 2014, 2016a, b) actively participated in the European consultations concerning the FTA with Malaysia, Myanmar, the Philippines, and Indonesia. The association pushed for an agreement that goes beyond WTO commitments in terms of reciprocal services liberalization for all parties. Another import-dependent group involved in car manufacturing, the European Tyre and Rubber Manufacturers' Association (2010), argued that the EU–Malaysia FTA ought to include a chapter on raw materials and that close attention to natural rubber trade should be paid when negotiating it.

European exporters, especially in the automotive, information and communication technologies, pharmaceuticals, agro-food, and beverages sectors, have considered ASEAN as a growing and attractive market (European Association of Automotive Suppliers 2012; European Commission 2016a). These industries called for the future trade agreements between the EU and ASEAN members to be in line with the FTAs concluded by the EU with Singapore and Vietnam. Furthermore, the European Services Forum (2016a) demanded greater market access to the Philippines for services and transparency in public procurement.

European exporters expressed their interest in protecting their competitiveness vis-à-vis other major international trade powers in the region. For instance, European car industries participating in the Commission's consultation for the EU–Philippines negotiations expressed a concern about the 'competitive disadvantage for EU business stemming from the PTAs' concluded by the Philippines with Japan, China, Australia, and New Zealand (European Commission 2016b). It is also important to note that Malaysia has autonomously implemented domestic reforms aimed at lifting trade and regulatory barriers to EU goods, services, and investments, in order to prepare to conclude a trade agreement with the EU.[13]

Finally, product-specific protectionist interests have lobbied the European Commission in order to affect the future PTAs with ASEAN members. The negotiations with Thailand have mobilized producers in the sugar sector, who have expressed concern about 'the expansive and aggressive nature of the Thai sugar industry', which in the eyes of these producers 'represents a serious threat to the EU sugar beet production and sugar sector in general' (International Confederation of European Beet Growers, CIBE 2013). A Baptist-bootlegger coalition involving agricultural organizations and environmental NGOs asked the Commission to include a clause in the EU–Malaysia trade agreement that would require Malay palm oil to conform to EU sustainability criteria (Poletti and Sicurelli 2016). The criteria on sustainability of palm oil are also one of the most controversial issues in the negotiations with Indonesia.[14]

The human rights implications of these agreements have not so far led to the mobilization of business and CSOs, except in the case of Myanmar. Industry associations such as the European Services Forum, Associazione Italiana Commercio Estero, and Green Power Energy Co. joined a network of NGOs, including EarthRights International, the FIDH and its member ALTSEAN-Burma, the Confédération des Syndicats Chrétiens (CSC), the Euro-Burma Office, and other human rights NGOs located in EU member states, to promote binding human rights norms in the trade agreement with Myanmar (European Commission 2013).

Since negotiations with ASEAN states are still ongoing and the European Commission has not published its negotiating positions, with the exception of that concerning the PTA with Indonesia (European Commission 2017), one may only speculate on the impact of the position papers of European stakeholders on the positions of the EU. These findings suggest that, despite differences in the income of the single ASEAN members and in trade flows with the EU, the European Commission is expected to promote high reciprocity in the liberalization commitments with its ASEAN partners and high standards of investment protection, government procurement, and sustainable development, modelled upon the EU–Vietnam deal.

The recent withdrawal of the US from the TPP under the Donald Trump administration made the EU a primary trade partner for each of the ASEAN members.[15] Following Trump's decision and MERCOSUR's common position on a trade deal with the EU in 2017, the EU also renewed its interest in an inter-regional deal with ASEAN (Euractiv 2017). This outlook is further reinforcing the expectation that the EU will try to negotiate trade agreements with the remaining ASEAN members building upon the model of the trade agreement with Vietnam.

Table 5.2 Political-economy dynamics in the trade negotiations with ASEAN countries

	Interest group mobilization for market access	*Domino effect*	*GVCs*
EU–ASEAN negotiations	• Import-dependent interests. • Exporters. • Investors. • Import-competing groups and NGOs.	• In 2002, ASEAN concluded a trade agreement with China and started free trade negotiations with the US. In the same year, EU started negotiating with ASEAN.	High integration of ASEAN members in the GVCs.
EU–Vietnam FTA	• Exporters and investors to Vietnam and ASEAN. • Import-dependent interests. • Import-competing interests (textiles, footwear, agriculture) and NGOs promoting EU regulatory standards.	• Singapore was the first ASEAN member that signed a trade agreement with the EU, in 2014, setting a benchmark for the EU–Vietnam deal. • Vietnam signed the TPP in 2015, contextually with the end of the EU–Vietnam negotiations.	Vietnam is highly integrated in the GVCs, and located downstream in high-tech manufacturing. Labour-intensive industry especially emerged in the textile, footwear, and agriculture sectors.

5.5 Conclusions

While formally driven by a concern to differentiate trade agreements according to the development needs of its partners and to a focus on the human rights implications of trade, the EU has mainly pursued economic interests in promoting an inter-regional deal with ASEAN and its member states. More specifically, it has promoted a trade agreement with Vietnam that provides the country with little flexibility in the promotion of liberalization and regulatory standards, while it takes a soft stance on human rights. The reasons behind this lack of coherence in the EU's approach to trade and development lie in the patterns of mobilization and impact of economic interest groups, and their relations with NGOs. The downstream location of Vietnam in high-tech manufacturing and its labour-intensive industry have empowered import-dependent and sector-specific import-competing groups. Competition with the US has also strengthened interests in protecting European exports and investments in the region. While NGOs found allies in the protectionist industry in the promotion of labour and environmental standards and strict enforcement procedures, they appeared less equipped to influence the European position concerning human rights.

On this basis, one can expect that the trade agreement will boost foreign investment in Vietnam and contribute to making it a production hub for the region. Nevertheless, the trade agreement fails in addressing a major priority of Vietnam's government, namely, that of upgrading Vietnam's position in GVCs. While one might expect progress through Vietnam's ratification and enforcement of sustainability standards, human rights dialogue largely remains confined to the diplomatic level.

The mobilization patterns that emerged in the negotiations with the Philippines and the text of the negotiating position adopted by the EU in the negotiations with Indonesia suggest that similar political-economy dynamics are going to permeate the ongoing negotiations with other South East Asian members and with ASEAN as a whole.

Notes

1. Interview, DG Trade, 16 July 2014.
2. Interview, Brussels, 16 July 2014.
3. Singapore has ratified all ILO fundamental conventions except the Freedom of Association and Protection of the Right to Organize

Convention (1948) and the Discrimination (Employment and Occupation) Convention (1985). Vietnam, in turn, has not ratified the Freedom of Association and Protection of the Right to Organize Convention, the Right to Organize and Collective Bargaining Convention (1949), and the Abolition of Forced Labour Convention (1957).

4. Interview, Eurocommerce, Brussels, 3 February 2009; Interview, Eurocommerce, Brussels, 10 January 2010.
5. Interview, Foreign Trade Association, Brussels, 13 February 2013.
6. Interviews, Commission officials, Brussels 7 January 2010, 7 April 2010, 14 February 2013.
7. Interview, 16 July 2014.
8. Interview, Assocalzaturifici, Milan, 1 July 2014.
9. Interview, DG Trade, 6 June Brussels 2014.
10. Interview, DG Trade, 16 July, Brussels 2014.
11. Interview, expert, Hanoi, 6 January 2015.
12. Interview, WTO Center Director, Hanoi, 17 February 2014.
13. Interview, European diplomat, 23 March 2017.
14. Interview, European diplomat, 13 June 2017.
15. Interview, European diplomat, 13 June 2017.

References

Borderlex. 2015. *EU Vietnam FTA: Rice Carve-Outs and 'Double Transformation' Rule of Origin in Sight.* 15 February. http://www.borderlex.eu/eu-vietnam-fta-devil-rule-origin/?print=print.

BusinessEurope. 2006. *UNICE Strategy on an EU Approach to Free Trade Agreements.* Brussels, 7 December.

———. 2007a. *BusinessEurope Position on the EU–Korea Free Trade Agreement—Position Paper.* Brussels, 18 July.

———. 2007b. *BusinessEurope Position on the EU–ASEAN Free Trade Agreement—Position Paper*. Brussels, 26 June.

CIBE 2013. *CIBE Working Document Answer to the Public Consultation on the FTA with Thailand*, D069-2013.

Doan, X. L. 2012. *Opportunities and Challenges in EU-ASEAN Trade Relations*, Report, EU Asia Center, 2 July. http://www.eu-asiacentre.eu/pub_details.php?pub_id=60. Accessed 25 Aug 2014.

Dreyer, A. 2015. *EU and Vietnam ink their FTA.* Borderlex. http://www.borderlex.eu/eu-vietnam-ink-fta/.

Eckhardt, J. 2011. Firm Lobbying and EU Trade Policy Making: Reflections on the Anti-Dumping Case Against Chinese and Vietnamese Shoes (2005–2011). *Journal of World Trade* 45 (5): 965–991.

———. 2015. *Business Lobbying and Trade Governance: The Case of EU-China Relations*. Basingstoke: Palgrave Macmillan.
Eckhardt, J., and A. Poletti. 2016. Trading with Asia: Import-Dependent Firms and EU-Asia Trade Agreements. *Journal of European Public Policy* 3 (10): 1543–1562.
EU Delegation to Vietnam. 2016. *Guide to the EU-Vietnam Free Trade Agreement*. June. http://trade.ec.europa.eu/doclib/docs/2016/june/tradoc_154622.pdf.
Euractiv. 2007. EU-ASEAN to Push for Trade Deal Despite Myanmar Discord. Brussels, 27 November.
———. 2015. *Hogan: EU-Vietnam Deal Won't Hurt Italian Rice*. Brussels, 28 August.
———. 2017. EU-ASEAN Trade Talks Show Signs of Life, 10 March.
Euratex. 2010. *Euratex: EU Trade Policy Revision—Position Paper*. Brussels.
Eurocommerce. 2007a. *Free Trade Negotiations EU–ASEAN: Contribution to the DG Trade Stakeholder Consultation*. Position Paper, Brussels, 31 May.
———. 2007b. Free Trade Negotiations EU–India: Contribution to the DG Trade Stakeholder Consultation. Position Paper, Brussels, 31 May.
———. 2009. *Eurocommerce Draft Action Plan*. Briefing to the Steering Committee, Brussels, 14 October.
———. 2010. *EU–Korea Trade Deal: A Boost for Retail and Wholesale*. Press Release, Brussels, 6 October.
———. 2012. *EU–Vietnam Trade*. Position Paper, Brussels, August 2012.
———. 2013. *EU-Thailand Free Trade Agreement—Eurocommerce Response to Consultation*. Position Paper, May.
———. 2015. *EU-Vietnam Trade: Commerce for Free Trade Agreement*. Briefing, Brussels, April.
European Association of Automotive Suppliers. 2012. *ASEAN—Policy Report*. Brussels, 26 September.
European Commission. 2006. *Global Europe: Competing in the World*. COM (2006) 567 Final, 4 October.
———. 2009. EU to Launch FTA Negotiations with Individual ASEAN Countries, Beginning with Singapore. Press Release, Brussels, 22 December.
———. 2013. Public Consultation on the Future Investment Relationship Between the EU and Myanmar. Results of the Questionnaire, Brussels, 15 July. http://trade.ec.europa.eu/consultations/index.cfm?consul_id=176.
———. 2015. *Facts and Figures: Free Trade Agreement Between EU and Vietnam—Fact Sheet*. Brussels, 04 August.
———. 2016a. *European Union, Trade in Goods with ASEAN*. Report, Brussels.
———. 2016b. *Questionnaire on a Free Trade Agreement with the Philippine Feedback from Industry Stakeholders*. Report, Brussels, 29 July. http://trade.ec.europa.eu/doclib/docs/2016/july/tradoc_154827.pdf.

———. 2017. The Texts Proposed by the EU for the Trade Deal with Indonesia. Brussels, 23 May. http://trade.ec.europa.eu/doclib/press/index.cfm?id=1620.
European Parliament. 2008. *Report on Trade and Economic Relations with the Association of Southeast Asian Nations.* Explanatory Statement.
———. 2009. *European Parliament Resolution of 26 November 2009 on the Situation in Laos and Vietnam*, P7_TA(2009)0104.
———. 2014. *The European Parliament's Role in Relations to Human Rights in Trade and Investment Agreements*, Directorate General for External Policies of the Union, Policy Department Study.
European Services Forum. 2006. *ESF Letter to Trade Commissioner Peter Mandelson on the External Aspects of Competitiveness.* Brussels, 21 March.
———. 2007. *ESF Position Paper on EU Free Trade Agreements.* Brussels 28 February.
———. 2011. *Bilateral Negotiations: EU-Malaysia.* Report.
———. 2014. Position Paper Submitted to the European Commission Public Consultation on the Future Investment Relationship Between the EU and Myanmar. Brussels, 15 February. http://trade.ec.europa.eu/consultations/index.cfm?consul_id=176.
———. 2016a. *ESF Response to DG Trade Questionnaire on the EU—Philippines FTA.* Press Release, 29 April.
———. 2016b. *Bilateral Negotiations: EU-Indonesia.* Report.
European Tyre and Rubber Manufacturers' Association. 2010. *ETRMA Contribution to a Consultation on the Free Trade Agreement with Malaysia.* Policy Report, 3 December.
Eurostat. 2015. *EU Trade and Investment Statistics with the Association of South East Asian Nations.* http://ec.europa.eu/eurostat/statistics-explained/index.php/EU_trade_and_investment_statistics_with_the_Association_of_South_East_Asian_Nations_(ASEAN).
Eurothon. 2012. *The EU Tuna Industry: Challenges and Prospects.* Conference Presentation. Bangkok, 24 May.
Foreign Trade Association. 2009. *European Retailers Call for Quick Conclusion to EU–Korea Free Trade Agreement.* Press Release, 23 February.
———. 2012. *EU–Vietnam Trade Negotiations.* Position Paper, 20 November.
———. 2014. *EU-Myanmar Trade Relations.* Position Paper, February. http://itp.fta-intl.org/resource/fta-position-paper-eu-myanmar-trade-relations-1-february-2014.
———. 2015. *FTA Welcomes the Opening of Negotiations Between Philippines and the EU.* Press Release, 22 December. http://itp.fta-intl.org/news/fta-welcomes-opening-negotiations-between-philippines-and-eu.
Garcìa, M. 2013. From Idealism to Realism? EU Preferential Trade Agreement Policy. *Journal of Contemporary European Research* 9 (4): 521–541.

Gavin, B., and A. Sindzingre. 2009. EU Trade Relations with Emerging Asia: Identifying the Issues. *Asia Europe Journal* 7 (1): 9–22.
Hoang, H.H. 2016. Normative Power Europe Through Trade: Vietnamese Perceptions. *International Relations* 30 (2): 176–205.
Hoang, H.H., and D. Sicurelli. 2017. The EU's Preferential Trade Agreements with Singapore and Vietnam. Market vs. Normative Imperatives. *Contemporary Politics* 23 (4): 369–387. https://doi.org/10.1080/13569775.2017.1289303.
Mallinder, L. 2008. *Shoemaker Fight Cheap Imports*. European Voice, 24 April.
Manger, M. 2012. Vertical Trade Specialization and the Formation of North–South PTAs. *World Politics* 64 (4): 622–658.
Meissner, K. 2016. A Case of Failed Interregionalism? Analyzing the EU-ASEAN Free Trade Agreement Negotiations. *Asia Europe Journal* 14 (3): 319–336.
Poletti, A., and D. Sicurelli. 2016. The European Union, Preferential Trade Agreements, and the International Regulation of Sustainable Biofuels. *Journal of Common Market Studies* 54 (2): 249–266.
Risoitaliano. 2015. *Stop Mr Hogan!* Press Release, 26 July.
Sahakyan, D. 2016. EU Trade Policy Responses to the Proliferation of Preferential Trade Agreements in Latin America and East and Southeast Asia. *Politics & Policy* 44 (1): 74–96.
Sicurelli, D. 2015a. The EU as a Promoter of Human Rights in Bilateral Trade Agreements: The Case of the Negotiations with Vietnam. *Journal of Contemporary European Research* 11 (2): 230–245.
———. 2015b. The EU as a Norm Promoter Through Trade. The Perceptions of Vietnamese Elites. *Asia Europe Journal* 13 (1): 23–39.

CHAPTER 6

Conclusions

Abstract This chapter summarizes the key findings of the book and discusses potential avenues for further research. The book's main findings can be summarized as follows. On the one hand, the comparison of the texts of the preferential trade agreements concluded by the EU with developing countries confirms the normative ambitions that characterize European trade policy. On the other hand, it shows that the EU has not consistently designed its trade agreements with a view to accommodate the development needs of its partners. The EU should be described as a selective normative power, namely, a trade power that prioritizes normative goals only when doing so is compatible with the demands of domestic coalitions of interest groups and NGOs. Different patterns of societal mobilization have characterized the domestic politics in the EU depending on the market access opportunities offered by negotiating partners, the presence of pre-existing trade agreements between those countries and major trade competitors of the EU, and the degree of integration of the trade partner in GVCs. These elements are major factors accounting for the different trade policy strategies the EU has pursued with different developing countries.

Keywords selective normative power • market access • trade competition • GVCs

A. Poletti, D. Sicurelli, *The Political Economy of Normative Trade Power Europe*, https://doi.org/10.1007/978-3-319-78864-7_6

The comparison between the trade agreements concluded by the EU with middle- and low-income countries has partially supported the European Commission's representation of the EU as a rather flexible and development-oriented trade actor, prone to accommodate the interests of its trade partners and differentiate trade commitments according to the level of development of its partners. Furthermore, by advocating the norms concerning sustainable development and human rights in the trade negotiations, EU trade policy has appeared consistent with its self-representation as an actor engaged in the promotion of its constitutive norms. Yet, our analysis also shows that the EU has adopted different approaches to development cooperation and norm promotion according to its trade partner, and that those variations only partially depend upon the development level of its trade partners. In other words, our analysis supports the view of the EU as a selective normative power.

The EU provided more favourable trade conditions to Sub-Saharan African countries, which represent the group with the higher percentage of least developed countries, than to Caribbean, Latin American, and South East Asian countries. It provided them with longer transition periods and accepted to negotiate goods-only trade agreements with those countries. At the same time, though, the analysis of trade agreements with Latin American, ACP, and ASEAN countries shows that the EU was not consistent in its commitment to norm promotion throughout the negotiations of different trade agreements. First, the EU treated Latin American and ASEAN countries differently, despite the fact that these countries share similar levels of socio-economic development. It conceded more flexibility in terms of transition periods and rules of origin to Latin American countries than to an ASEAN country such as Vietnam. Second, it promoted the most stringent norms concerning sustainable development and human rights in the EPAs with the ACP countries, despite fierce opposition of African negotiators. It adopted a more explicit language concerning suspension of reciprocal trade commitments in case of human rights violations in the trade agreements with Latin American countries, while it promoted a more detailed consultation procedure in the enforcement of sustainable development norms in the trade agreement with Vietnam.

This analysis shows that the EU has pursued the objective of tailoring its trade policy to the 'development needs' of its trade partners in a context characterized by the powerful political constraints defined by the preferences and patterns of political mobilization of key domestic constituencies. Our analysis therefore demonstrates that the EU is able to operate as a normative trade power only insofar as doing so is compatible with the demands that organized economic interests and CSOs channel through the EU trade policymaking process. The EU appears as a trade actor permeable to pressures of economic interest groups and NGOs. More specifically, our study shows that, as assumed by the mainstream political-economy literature, organized groups' demands to increase access to foreign markets played a key role in shaping EU trade policy strategies towards different developing regions and countries alongside the normative concerns expressed by various European CSOs. They did so by advocating agreements that would minimize the potential negative distributive effects of opening up the EU market to increased foreign imports, to offset the negative distributive implications of trade policy initiatives of other major trading powers, and to respond to the incentives brought about by the growing integration of the EU in GVCs.

Negotiations with Latin American countries mainly mobilized European exporter interest, aiming to creating a level playing field with US exporters. These groups effectively pushed EU policymakers to obtain market access conditions in CA and the AC similar to those enjoyed by their US counterparts as a result of the trade agreements signed between them and the US a few years earlier. A domino effect was also detected in the negotiations with Vietnam, due to the parallel negotiations of the TPP. Yet, the high level of integration of the EU and South East Asian counties' economies in the context of GVCs explains the key political role played by organized groups representing the interests of European import-dependent firms in these negotiations. The EU adapted its proposal on transition periods and market access to the deal negotiated by Vietnam within the TPP. The position of the European Commission on rules of origin, instead, accommodated preferences of import-dependent firms, while also seeking to respond to the demands of protectionist interests. Finally, negotiations with ACP countries, a set of countries that is neither integrated in GVCs nor central in the dynamics of economic competition between the EU and the US, have mainly mobilized NGOs and protectionist agricultural interests. Service interest groups also lobbied the European Commission in order to shape its negotiating position with the CARIFORUM. In the absence of offensive interests of the European industry in the EPAs negotiations, NGOs proved especially influential in promoting long transition periods for the liberalization of trade with the Sub-Saharan African countries, while protectionist interests managed to obtain protection for key European agricultural products, most notably sugar.

The stringent human rights and sustainable development norms promoted by the EU in the EPAs seem to confirm the hypothesis that when there are no relevant commercial interests at stake and the asymmetric relationship between the EU and the partner is high, the EU is more prone to act as a normative power. On the contrary, when the economic stakes are high, key economic business constituencies, such as exporters, importers, and import competitors, manage to play a key role in the politics of trade policymaking in the EU. This does not mean that traditional market access and normative concerns should necessarily be at odds with each other. In fact, these two sets of priorities may end up being compatible. For instance, the inclusion of provisions requiring developing partners to ensure high standards of labour and environmental protection in these trade agreements often addresses the pressures of both organized economic interests, which have an interest in exporting costly regulatory standards or reducing negative externalities that different domestic regulatory practices can generate, and CSOs, which defend a progressive agenda within which these issues usually figure prominently. At the same time, our analysis shows that normative concerns are somewhat residual in the making of EU trade policy, namely, they can be pursued only to the extent that they are compatible with the underlying political constraints defined by the key economic interests that these trade negotiations touch upon.

In light of these findings, a number of challenges can be identified for the EU attempts to play a normative power role in ongoing and future trade negotiations. First, it remains to be seen whether the EU will be able to conclude coherent regional deals with MERCOSUR, ASEAN, and the remaining Sub-Saharan regions that have not yet concluded an EPA with the EU. Given the lack of consistency between trade and development objectives in the trade agreements between African groups of states and between Vietnam, on the one hand, and Singapore, on the other hand, the objective of promoting inter-regional deals appears overtly ambitious. Second, and in the longer run, differences in the degree of normative commitment that the EU has demonstrated in trade negotiations with a single trade partner still affect its ambition to set the basis for future multilateral commitments in the context of the WTO. Finally, it remains to be seen whether, irrespective of existing differences in these agreements' provisions, EU trade policy strategies will prove successful in promoting development through trade. It is too early to comment on the development impact of the trade agreements analysed in this volume. An assessment of EU trade agreements' potential to foster development ultimately depends on whether they will be instrumental in enabling its trade partners to maximize their ability to ripen the potential benefits of a deeper integration in global markets. This means that an assessment of the normative character of EU trade policy towards developing countries and regions will have to incorporate analyses of the extent to which EU trade agreements promoted an upgrading of their positions in GVCs, stimulated a diversification of their exports, and contributed to making them more attractive for international investments.

Index

A. Poletti, D. Sicurelli, *The Political Economy of Normative Trade Power Europe*, https://doi.org/10.1007/978-3-319-78864-7